The Promised Land Dachshund Sanctuary

A Story of Rescue and Redemption

Connie Eicher

"To watch one Dachshund regain his strength and self-esteem, rejuvenates our souls and reinforces our efforts."

D0055131

Foreword by Jessica J.E. Smith
Edited by Jessica J.E. Smith, Gaye White, and Lilia Castillo

"They say it takes a special person to open their heart and home to those less fortunate. In this case, it is two special hearts that have combined to open a new world of love, friendship, and security to many abandoned souls. Connie and Rick Eicher have dedicated themselves to a journey that most of us will never know. A journey that begins with a deep look into the eyes of an innocent creature whose life has suddenly changed. Eyes that could tell stories of pain, misfortune, neglect, heartache, and sadness.

I have had the pleasure of knowing many of the rescues that have crossed the path of the Promised Land Dachshund Sanctuary. Each unique and special in their own being, everyone of them has touched my heart with their strong spirit of life and love. I have seen these little seedlings blossom into the most remarkable creatures under the guidance of Connie and Rick. To be able to be part of their lives and share in their journey will forever hold a special place in my heart.

There are not enough words to describe the commitment that Connie and Rick have given to these wonderful creatures and will give to the ones yet to come. They know not what "no" is, but rather hold open arms for any that need them. Their kindness and generosity can fill hearts big and small; human and non; and for this, they walk a path followed and loved by so many. Thank you for all you do."

—*Dr. Jessica Todia DVM*

To all the dogs across this country still waiting to be rescued and to my husband, Rick, who intends to help get it done.

At the End of the Day

By Jessica J.E. Smith

What if this week never ends? Barking, barking, and more barking. The dogs would bark, and we would say, "How high?" We trudged through morning chores, with permanent looks of misery upon our faces, and counted the minutes until we could escape to a more peaceful seclusion without the constant hounding of the hounds.

This quiet reverie would be short lived, as the mutts wait on no one. They all needed exercise, and medicine had to be given every few hours. Learning all of their names was not the hardest part, although it seemed the most frustrating. The most difficult of it all was certainly keeping our patience. Winston Churchill once said, "When you are going through hell, keep going." We felt that this was the motto of our week, and that if we stuck to it there would indeed be an end to the madness.

One afternoon, I tried to take a nap, but soon discovered that this was much easier dreamed about than done. With each dog vying for a spot where they would be curled up next to me, I was shortly jilted from my efforts to rest.

As each day progressed to the inevitable dimness of evening, I wondered just when it was that my parents had lost their minds, and what, if anything, I could do to help them find their sanity once more. As I pondered this question, we dove into evening chores. Before putting the dogs to bed, we would retreat to the sanctity of the almost tranquil back porch.

And, at the end of the day it finally hit me: this was all worth it.

I looked up from my spot on the hanging porch swing, and I saw Charlie digging up his dirt. I remembered how many times Mom called me after he got Kennel Cough, and how worried she was. I remember her telling me how heartbroken Daddy was and how the vet wasn't sure that Charlie was going to make it. I knew that Charlie was one of his favorites, and if they lost Charlie from this disease, it would hurt him deeply. Daddy pulls each little critter he loves into a special place in his heart. This place holds them forever, with all the heartache and happiness they experience together. I have seen him lose a friend given to him in the form of a dog, and I have felt that same pain in my life. I knew the devastation it would cause, so I hoped and prayed that Charlie would recover.

And here I was, at the end of the day, watching Charlie dig the dirt from one end of the flower bed to the other, only to move it back once again. He recovered to regain his old pizzazz, and I couldn't help but grin at the serenity of it all. I finally saw that my parents had indeed found a happiness that is extremely rare and certainly unique. At the end of the day, I envied them their joy.

Our daughter, Jessica, wrote this in 2003 after taking on our sanctuary for a full week, allowing her father and me to take a much needed vacation.

Acknowledgements

Many earthly angels came into our lives over the years. One of the first and most important helped me put together a website. Kate worked countless hours creating, maintaining, and updating our online presence. We flooded that site with pictures and news of our residents. And just in the nick of time, we began to receive much needed donations. While these donations never covered our monthly expenses, they allowed us to continue our work.

Gaye began to make and send thirty to forty beautiful, crocheted blankets each year. To this day, fifteen years after we started, she still sends new blankets every year at Christmas time.

Our daughter Jessica and her husband Billy took over the entire sanctuary for the only week long vacation Rick and I have taken together in the last fifteen years. Our niece Jordon spent many hours after school and on weekends playing with the dogs and helping me clean. Charlotte helped me to coordinate transports and to build our network of rescuers and donors. She once coordinated a four part transport of a senior dog from New York State all the way to our sanctuary in West Texas. Cindy, Michelle, Greg, Misti, Linné, Pam, Kathy, Paul, Tammy, Shelly, Barb and Mike, Dee, Barbara, Ellen, Pat, Christine, Kathleen, Donna, Glenda, Mitzi, and Melle Belle make up the short list of additional people that made our efforts successful. Many more go unnamed but never forgotten.

The contributions of the many members of our support team included, but were not limited to, transport assistance, financial subsidies, equipment and food donations, fund raising efforts, dog sitting, bathing dogs, playing with dogs, cleaning yards, washing blankets, home checks, background checks, answering emails, and consoling Rick and me in times of loss.

A good veterinarian proved to be one of our biggest assets. We didn't strike gold with the first one we tried. The policies adhered to by our first vet did not match our goals and didn't allow any consideration of our charitable work. We all received a true blessing the day I found Dr. Jessica Todia at A-Z Vet Clinic. She and I sat down one day in her waiting room and discussed our efforts and our needs. She immediately offered easy access and considerations that allowed us to stretch our monthly budgets to cover the necessities.

We still use Doc Jess exclusively for our dogs. We are friends, and she lives right down the road. She runs a rescue of her own that specializes in birds and reptiles but takes in all sorts of creatures. Doc Jess not only grieves with us when we lose a dog, she also donates to many charitable causes that fund research of animal diseases. She does so in the name of the dogs that her clients lose. Once, she even came to our house at midnight, in her pajamas, to euthanize a badly injured dog in pain. Her dedication is limitless, and we love her. You will find her name sprinkled throughout the last fourteen years of our story.

Another very important character in our lives is Christy Vaughn Eicher. She is a beautiful, black and tan, miniature Dachshund. Rick had Christy I and II as a child. He remembers fondly the day his Dad brought his first Christy puppy home in his pocket. We acquired Christy III, early in our marriage. Sadly, she came to us with distemper and did not live past eight weeks of age. Christy IV became part of our family while we still lived in town. She remained with us for thirteen years. This Christy survived parvovirus as an adult dog only because of Rick's dedication over several horrible nights to keep her hydrated. Christy V came into our lives after we moved to the country, and she was nineteen years old when she succumbed to a brain tumor. Her picture is featured on the cover of this book. We currently have Christy VI, the undisputed queen of our sanctuary. She is nine years old, and we feel she is the culmination of all the Christy dogs that have come before her. Christy's influence is the reason we rescue primarily Dachshunds.

God blessed our lives when He put the desire to rescue dogs into our hearts. His will and His love for all creatures has been our biggest inspiration.

Table of Contents

Introduction

Rescuing dogs has always come naturally to us. Most of the dogs we have owned came from local shelters or off the streets. Rick grew up loving Dachshunds, and I always had a German Shepherd by my side. Several dogs of both breeds shared our home and our lives while we raised our kids. Once we moved to our country home, the possibility to help more dogs increased dramatically. With our children both gone to college in 2001, we decided to begin an official rescue organization.

We named our rescue "The Promised Land Dachshund Sanctuary." It was our intention to rescue senior and special-needs Dachshunds, who often fell through the cracks of the ever expanding rescue community. These dogs required specialized care and would take up a scarce spot in most rescuers' capacity, with little chance of adoption. While we understood the need to rescue as many dogs as possible, our hearts could not bear the thought of some of the dogs most in need getting left behind.

One of my first rescue buddies, Christine, advised us to set a limit on the number of dogs we could care for at one time. We set our first limit at twenty, and busted through that boundary in less than three months. Our occupancy maxed out in the summer of 2004 at fifty-seven dogs. The needs of the sanctuary often extended beyond the capacity of our finances. But, we never ran out of space, and we never ran out of desire to help as many dogs as possible. Blessings from above, Rick's tireless work habits, donations, and fund raising helped us bridge the gaps in our finances.

Once the word spread that we could and would accept special-needs Dachshunds, our name became familiar to rescuers throughout the southern United States. Often, we made a deal with other rescuers to take an un-adoptable dog from them, while they took one or more of our young and healthy residents. Before long the transport of dogs to and from the sanctuary became a huge part of my life. My brother David, a disabled vet, traveled with me, and we burned up the roads all over Texas, New Mexico, and Arizona. Our little Ford Explorer wore out numerous sets of tires and often needed monthly oil changes. Rick worked as many hours as he could to pay the expenses and repair the car when needed.

Our home changed to accommodate the needs of our dogs. All the carpet throughout the house was removed, and our living room soon held rows of kennels. Several rooms of the house acquired gates and/or doggie doors. The back fence received some repairs and new gates. Rick eventually divided the backyard into two sections. We enclosed our big back porch and installed a wood burning stove for heat. Other plans for renovations of our home were mostly put on hold to accommodate the needs of the dogs. Now, thankfully, we have begun to mesh the needs of our old home for repair and renovation with the needs of the dogs we love.

All of these considerations made for the sake of the dogs created challenges where our family life was concerned. None of those obstacles have been insurmountable, however. Our children, and now our grand-children, understand our commitment to this cause and have supported our efforts from the beginning.

Only recently, and after much public outcry, have our local shelters begun to make an effort to go no-kill. When we first opened our sanctuary in 2001, the numbers of dogs euthanized within a forty mile radius of our home broke our hearts. Many of our dogs came from these shelters. Our hearts demanded that we do more to help bring down those shameful numbers, and on occasion that meant rescuing outside our chosen breed of Dachshunds.

Our policies at the sanctuary have always been simple. First and fore-most, all dogs must be spayed or neutered as soon as possible. We refuse to add to the overpopulation of dogs in our area. Twice during the last fifteen years, we rescued pregnant dogs. The first pregnant dog we acquired could not safely give birth to the huge puppies she carried, and her pup-pies had already perished when we had her spayed. The other pregnant rescue, Jodie, gave birth the first night she spent at the sanctuary.

The next policy that we have managed to adhere to almost without exception, is a pack therapy theory. Dogs are social animals. To Rick and me that means that they benefit tremendously from socializing with one another. They comfort each other, they entertain each other, and they distract each other from grief, pain, or illness. Several rescuers scoffed at that idea. They felt we endangered our dogs by allowing them to live as one large pack.

There have been times over the years when our dogs all living together caused some situations that needed additional consideration. On a few occasions we made the decision to extend an initial isolation period to accommodate an especially difficult dog. There have even been a few instances where we quickly transferred a dog to another rescuer because of the needs of our more fragile dogs. We still feel the benefits realized from the pack life far outweigh the liabilities. We have expanded over the years to five separate areas where we keep our dogs. This gives us more options when a new dog comes into our lives, but none of our dogs lives alone.

Our final policy concerns dogs that are completely devoted to each other. These dogs formed their own family, and we refuse to break those families apart, even when it means healthy, adoptable dogs will remain at the sanctuary.

The dogs taught us everything we needed to know to care for them. Some lessons struck us harder than others. We learned that every dog has unique needs, unique personalities, and unique quirks. We learned that every dog added something to our lives and increased our respect for all life. We learned that dogs grieve and sometimes that grief consumes their health. We learned pure joy outweighs many of the difficulties from an effort such as ours. We learned that heartache can propel us forward if we allow our hearts to remain open.

The rescue community taught us a lot about human nature. Most people contribute to the care of abandoned animals out of love. Some rescuers are capable of handling the most complicated projects, while others are best suited to working out the details. While some people can present more obstacles than bridges, all people can contribute to the effort. The charitable condition in the heart is capable of expanding, if allowed.

Rick and I also learned a few things about each other over the years. Our abilities differed in several ways. Rick can soothe and befriend almost any distraught animal if given the time. I've seen him do it with dogs, cats, horses, goats, rabbits, emus, an abandoned bobcat, ground squirrels, and even mice. *Yikes!* Rick shines in the entertainment aspect of our care. He has always been the one to throw the ball and to pile up in the yard with twenty dogs covering his body. I am better suited for dealing with the stress of walking the shelters or holding an ill dog while we carry out the last, and often most important decision, to end their pain. We learned that together, we are capable of moving mountains, one little furry creature at a time.

Chapter 1
Alpha Male

Our first official rescue came in the form of a skinny, red Dachshund with sunken eyes and very little energy. André had been on the streets, and the wear showed in his eyes. It was thrilling and addicting to watch him come into his own after only a few weeks of the kind of care he deserved. André became our alpha male, not only because he arrived first, but because he soon blossomed into a curious, playful, lovable leader. He was approximately one year old when I brought him home from the local shelter in July of 2001.

One afternoon, a few weeks after André arrived, I came home with a carload of groceries. Rick helped me bring them all inside, and I got busy putting everything away. I soon discovered that André was nowhere to be found. We repeatedly went through the yard and the entire house, growing more panicked with each passing moment. When we couldn't find André after searching everywhere, we questioned whether he might have had an opportunity to slip out the front door.

Panic soon turned to desperation, and we both jumped into our cars to search the area. When the sun set and twilight began to steal our ability to see, we knew our chances of finding him dwindled. But we drove on for several more hours, calling his name through the night, hoping we might get lucky. Finally, exhaustion and grief took hold, and we had to concede our search. Somehow we managed to get our evening tasks done and settled in to try and distract ourselves in front of the television. By the time we turned out the lights to face a sleepless night, we were both speechless with worry.

I have no idea how long we laid there in the silence, when I heard Rick get up and go into the kitchen. Then he yelled, "André!" I bolted out of bed to find Rick sitting in the middle of the floor with André on his lap. Rick explained he heard a faint whimpering sound and went into the kitchen to determine its origin. He pulled open a bottom cabinet, and André walked out stretching his back legs after what had apparently been a nice, long nap. André got into that cabinet while I put the groceries away. I still can't believe he slept through our frantic search of the house, all that time we spent in our cars, and an hour or so of staring at the television screen. Relief hardly describes the way we felt when we took our first deep breath in hours. Rick and I eventually got some sleep that night; André lay between us on the bed with our arms around him.

Within thirty days we rescued eight more Dachshunds. Three of those new dogs came to us under the age of five. Eddie, Freddie, and Brandi Lee were immediately recruited by André to join his new club. Those four dogs became the quintessential gang of rowdy teenagers. Led by André, they ran and wrestled for hours each day. They could often be found together in the yard, and whatever André started, they all participated in. We nicknamed them the Rat Pack.

Rick and I agreed after rescuing André that as our first he was going to remain with us at the sanctuary. After one failed attempt to adopt Eddie and Freddie together, they also joined the ranks of our permanent

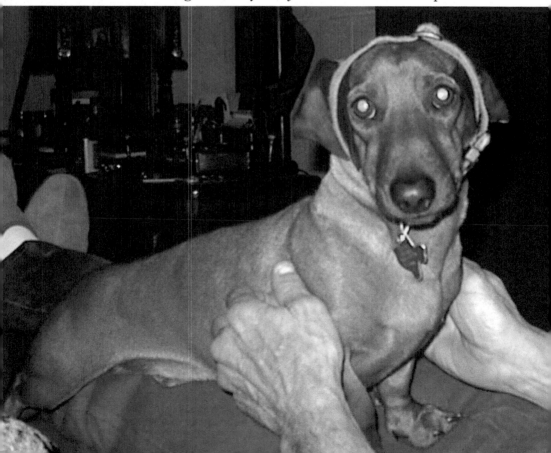

residents. Brandi Lee, as a mixed breed, never received any attention on the website, and her moody disposition made a placement difficult to say the least. The Rat Pack stayed together, dominating the activities around here for quite a few years.

André is fearless and silly. He has never shied away from any dog, large or small, any humans, or any loud noises. One day I noticed him standing a few feet from the doggie door in the kitchen. A storm approached from the west, and the thunder had just started rolling through the sky. All the other dogs scrambled for cover. André waited until everyone came in, and he walked slowly and deliberately out the doggie door. I watched through the kitchen window as he placed himself in the middle of the yard, and raised his head to the sky. One lightening bolt after another cracked from the dark clouds above him. He stood like a statue, staring up at the one thing that most of our dogs were deadly afraid of. *I halfway expected him to pound his chest and yell, "I am André, Alpha Male!"*

I can think of only one thing in Andrés life that upsets him: that is the tick and flea drops we use to keep pests off our dogs. André runs and hides. Several of our dogs try to get away from me, but André is the only one that tries to hide. Maybe he thinks because I have so many other dogs to treat I will forget about him if he finds the perfect hideaway. The funny thing is, André hides in the same spot every time. And that spot is behind one of the large pecan trees in the corner of the yard. It's obvious he hasn't thought things through; his head sticks out on one side of the tree, and his tail sticks out on the other.

André has enjoyed almost perfect health for fifteen years. He needed some occasional dental work, and at the age of six he went down in his back. Doc Jess said the X-rays didn't show any permanent damage. With steroids and kennel rest, André would soon be back to normal. While André did not necessarily enjoy being confined to a kennel, he reacted better than most dogs in the same situation. André always had one of his favorite chew toys with him, and he took great pains to arrange his blanket to suit his needs.

In the evening hours, Rick took his kennel to the back porch, and André watched the other dogs in the yard. The degree of activity never rose to its usual level during those weeks. The Rat Pack didn't play when André was away, but everyone celebrated the day André came out of his kennel with a healthy back.

At the age of sixteen, André has seen so much. He personally greeted over two hundred fifty dogs that came through our doors. He watched blind and deaf puppies learn to play, and he watched old timers face their final hours. He watched very ill dogs return to health and vitality, and

he watched disabled dogs learn to love their new lives. He watched his playground become covered in hail stones, deep drifts of snow, downed tree limbs, sheets of ice, and piles of sand that blew in with our harsh West Texas winds. Andrés life has been full of love, attention, good food, excellent vet care, over thirty-five hundred days of beautiful sunshine, and more friends than we can all remember.

André is getting old now. His face and most of his body is covered with gray, and his step has lost its enthusiasm. He often finds himself in unfamiliar places, even though his environment remains the same. André doesn't run and play anymore and pays scant attention to those who do. He still enjoys world class scratching sessions with Rick, and he knows he can get a lick off the peanut butter spoon when I give meds each morning. He has a favorite spot on his pillow on the floor during the day and on the bed at night. Every evening, when André cuddles in for a good night's sleep, Rick and I pray for just one more day.

Chapter 2

The Blind Leading the Blind

We had only been rescuing for a few months when we received a call about a white Dachshund that needed a home. At that point, we had never heard of a white Dachshund, and we were intrigued. Our contact in San Angelo told us that this little, double dapple female was six months old, blind and deaf. She had spent the first months of her life alone in a backyard because the owners did not know how to deal with her disabilities. It took Rick and me all of ten minutes to discuss the situation and decide we wanted to give this little gal a spot in our sanctuary. We felt sure we were equipped to deal with any impairment thrown at us. *Yeah right!*

By 10:30 the next morning David and I were in San Angelo picking up this new puppy. Shortly after we arrived, our rescue friend, Pat, pulled into the designated meeting place and got out of her car. Her drawn face and tired eyes caught me slightly off guard. I greeted her as she opened the back hatch of her SUV. The shrill sound that blasted our ears raised the hair on the back of my neck. Pat pulled the puppy out of the kennel and I got my first look at Xera Mae.

Her long, slender head and white body resembled a rat with slightly longer legs. As I took her into my arms, she scratched and clawed at me to get as high up on my shoulder as she could. The shriek coming from her four pound body pierced my ears, and I soon learned that she had done nothing in the last twenty-four hours but scream. After placing her in the kennel in the back of my car, I assured Pat that Xera would be fine. Pat relaxed a bit when I closed my hatch, and I realized she had been afraid I might change my mind about accepting this dog into my care.

The drive home took about two hours. Normally, David and I enjoyed a jovial and lively conversation. Unfortunately, Xera let it be known that there would be no discussion in that car. The first hour of the drive frightened me; I couldn't stop thinking about how Rick and I were going to handle this little megaphone. All our previous rescues had settled in, and rested in the kennel during the drive home. Not Xera! The second hour, my emotions escalated to a frantic state as the interior of the car seemed to shrink with each passing mile. David's face had a painted on half smile, but his white knuckles holding the arm rest assured me that his nerves were as frazzled as mine. The last few minutes of our trip broke my heart. It sunk in just how unhappy this little dog really was. David almost waited until the car came to a complete stop in front of his house before he leaped out, waved good-bye, and hurried inside. A few minutes later I stood outside my car, frozen with fear. *What had we gotten ourselves into?*

For the next twenty-four hours, Xera continued to screech. A strident, piercing wail that was somewhere between a baby crying and a boiling tea kettle filled our home. There was no making her happy. Holding her didn't help. Kenneling her didn't help. Walking with her didn't help. Rick tried to soothe her with the comfort of his strong hands around her, but that didn't help either. Up to this point in our rescue experience, we had watched with wonder and admiration as each newcomer to the sanctuary had been comforted and supported by the other dogs. The pack therapy had worked wonders for everyone until Xera entered our world. The other dogs were certainly interested in her, but when they came close enough for her to smell, she escalated her squalls and added to the growing number of scratches on our arms and necks.

The nighttime hours of that first day are a bit of a blur in my memory now. I do remember taking Xera to a back bedroom and lying with her on the bed. As exhausted as we were, I struggled to hold her against me, and thankfully she finally gave it up; we both slept a few hours. I woke up early the next morning to the sound of her hitting the floor, followed immediately by her cranking up her vocal chords again.

Throughout that day, I held her as much as I could, but I also had to care for the other dogs. As a result she spent some of her time hollering from a kennel on our dresser. By the time Rick got home, my nerves were strung tight and ready to pop. Rick suggested that we try introducing Gracie, by herself, to Xera. Gracie had proven her expertise in soothing the most frightened and shy newcomers, and we hoped this wasn't beyond her talents.

We placed Xera on the ground next to Gracie, and her relentless screams changed pitch a bit. She began to spin. She ran a circle about two feet in diameter, at full speed, never reducing the volume of her cries. Gracie appeared totally disinterested in this strange white dog. She waddled around outside Xera's circle, inspecting doggie beds and toys on the floor. No doubt she was compiling her subtle strategy to approach this particularly perplexing patient. And then she made her move. She stepped directly into the path of Xera's relentless circle. Xera ran smack into Gracie's side, and she finally stopped screaming. Gracie stood perfectly still for several moments while Xera smelled her from head to toe. Xera returned to her spinning, but only for a few turns until Gracie stepped again into her circle, and they collided again. To our complete surprise, once Xera familiarized herself with the smell of our little Florence Nightingale, she stood still and quiet while Gracie acclimated herself with our new addition.

Xera spent the next hour or so exploring our bedroom. Gracie sidled up to her several times and stood just close enough for Xera to get her scent. When confronted with a new doggie bed or toy that no doubt held a slew of different doggie aromas, Xera went back to her spinning until Gracie again stepped into her path. Rick and I watched in humble amazement as Gracie, a cancer survivor given up as too ill to have any quality to her life, helped Xera, a blind and deaf puppy with no social skills, begin to accept and adapt to her new world. That night Xera and Gracie slept together in a kennel and a glorious, restful silence blanketed our sanctuary.

For the next few days we reintroduced one after another of our pack to Xera. With Gracie by her side, Xera accepted each new dog as readily as they accepted her. Within a week Xera began to sleep in our bed with us… and a few other scoundrels.

Patience, experimentation, and the ever present Gracie were the only tools at our disposal to teach Xera how to thrive in our sanctuary. It took us both a few weeks to stop trying to deal with Xera by talking to her. Once she was familiar with the entire pack, we began to introduce her to the other areas of the sanctuary. Her exploration was methodical and becoming more predictable with each new environment. She gave way to anyone crossing her path and learned to avoid the dogs that were less likely to tolerate her routine.

Xera used her sense of smell to make up for her loss of sight and hearing, so we tried to use that as our teaching tool. One day, Rick and I knelt down on each side of the doggie door and took turns blowing on her through the opening. We hoped to encourage her to step through, and eventually she did. When Xera learned to use that doggie door, her freedom and confidence grew tremendously.

More than with any of our other special-needs dogs, knowledge, both for Xera and for us, came in spurts. New smells would often send her into a spin. At first, we tried to intervene, thinking that she was upset and needed comforting. While this worked, it wasn't always doable; Xera needed to be more independent. Eventually, we realized that she used that spin to check out her immediate environment and set her perimeters. Xera learned that if she combined a spin with a shriek, she could get attention. *Being blind and deaf did not make her dumb!*

Not long after Xera became comfortable at the sanctuary, our daughter Jessica visited from college. She decided to see how Xera would respond to a bath. She received astonishing results. Xera pawed at the water with a sideways motion, as if to move it like sand. She dropped her head close to the water and then pulled it back up again. She was apparently trying to focus on this wondrous new discovery. Jessica and I watched her, thrilled with the obvious joy in her reactions. Xera kneaded that water until it got cold. She never got wet above her belly, but she did not spin. And she did not scream. Xera actually played that day for the first time.

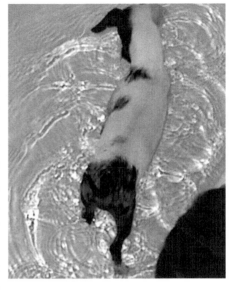

Soon, we happened upon one of Xera's other passions: plastic bottles. She found plastic jugs of water in the back of our SUV while we were on a trip across the state. Unfortunately, by the time we discovered her new obsession, two gallon jugs of water sat empty in a puddle on the carpet. She became so adept at manipulating all kinds of plastic bottles, that she could run through the doggie door with an empty gallon milk jug in her mouth and not touch either side of the opening. Water hoses also began to suffer her wrath, especially if they were turned on. Many times she was guilty of picking up a hose and squirting the other dogs with it, *accidentally, of course*. Her sister, Opal Ann, who came to us several months after Xera, occasionally fell victim to hose attacks. Xera

absolutely loved the kiddie pool in the backyard: playing in the water for hours, walking the edge of the pool, and examining the contents. Her never ending exploration of the element it contained delighted Rick and me.

Anyone that has ever owned more than one dog at a time knows that they will develop a pecking order. When you have thirty to fifty dogs, the status of each dog can be quite complicated. Some dogs are more dominant about food, while others will get first choice of sleeping spots. Xera never had much sway in the yard. But she soon discovered a true source of power: the darkness under the covers at night. She had her favorite spot, and she struck out with amazing accuracy at anyone who intruded. We wondered if she somehow sensed that the lack of light provided an equalizer for her, or maybe she drew her line at losing her spot on the bed.

Double dapples almost always have numerous congenital maladies. Xera, like all special-needs dogs, never realized she was disabled. She was vibrant, extremely active, and lived a full and happy life with us for eleven years. Then, sadly, her organs betrayed her. Our hearts broke the day our little white bombshell crossed the Rainbow Bridge. *I wonder how long it took her to discover the path to the water under that bridge.*

Chapter 3

A Nurse, an Athlete, and a Miner

A nurse, an athlete, and a miner, walked into a bar...Well actually they walked into our hearts in a way that we could have never expected.

A Nurse

Gracie was five years old when she came to the sanctuary as a cancer survivor. Her original owners did not feel they could bear to watch her suffer. They turned her over to a local Dachshund rescue. As a special-needs Dachshund, it didn't take her long to make her way to our door. Her cancer had been in her thyroid gland, and after surgery she took meds every day. Giving medicine to our little furry friends did not present a problem for us. We covered the pills with peanut butter, and the dogs clamored for their turn at the medicine counter.

A black and tan short hair, Gracie was soft, cuddly, and over-weight. Her movements were slow and preconceived. Her coat reminded me of rabbit fur, so velvety and smooth you couldn't resist stroking it. And Gracie certainly got her fair share of strokes.

In the evenings after all my chores were done, I often sat on the bed and watched television with the dogs coming and going as they pleased. Most of our pack had a special place they liked to rest, and Gracie's place was right by my side. She knew the loving was easy to come by there, and she never resisted a chance to stock up. Like most Dachshunds, Gracie barked at any sign or sound out of the ordinary. She had been with us for several weeks when I noticed something that had not come to my attention before. One evening as I relaxed on the bed, Gracie climbed the ramp and sat down on the end of the bed. She surveyed the location of all the little bodies already comfortable around me, then suddenly jumped to her feet and barked wildly at the door.

With an average of thirty Dachshunds in our home, Rick and I had stopped worrying every time the dogs barked. But the perceived peril lurking in the dark concerned the dogs. Everyone on the bed jumped up and ran barking towards the danger Gracie discovered.

Gracie waited until all the dogs vacated the bed and ran through the house. Then she slowly made her way to the place she wanted all along: right beside me. The next evening, the events repeated themselves exactly the same way. Day after day, I knew what was coming when Gracie showed up on the foot of the bed. But interestingly enough, the other dogs didn't realize this particular invisible intruder showed up each night at about the same time. Gracie never failed to get her spot.

Several months after Grace arrived, we got a call about a double dapple Dachshund puppy born partially blind. Patch was very tiny and looked extremely vulnerable in our pack of full grown dogs. I worried she would be an easy mark for some of the more cantankerous older dogs, as well as some of the rougher and rowdier young males in our group. She was only seven weeks old.

Everyone that saw her fell in love, including Gracie. For several days after Patch arrived, I put her in a crate when I had to run errands. I noticed one day when I came home that Gracie sat on the floor next to Patch's crate. She wanted "her" puppy. So the next afternoon, when we all enjoyed the sunshine and the wading pool, I kept my eye on Gracie. She walked around thoughtlessly, acting like she wasn't paying attention to anything or anyone. But every time I looked at Gracie, she hovered within a few feet of Patch.

Later that evening, while checking my email, I looked across the room and saw Gracie and Patch. Gracie had lain down. Patch crawled up on her back and slipped over the top until her head rested on the ground. Her body and feet remained strewn over Gracie's back. At first I thought our little nurse looked a bit unhappy, but soon I realized Gracie was exactly where she wanted to be. She made no effort to move, and Patch enjoyed a long nap in comfort on Gracie's soft back.

Over the years, Rick and I came to trust in Gracie as our nurse and our

welcoming party. Any newcomer to the pack could expect to find Gracie close by for the first few days. Any special-needs dog could count on Gracie to be their guide and their security blanket. We watched Gracie on more than one occasion get between a vulnerable dog and the rowdy younger dogs. She used her body to push a new dog into a corner, to keep it corralled and safe.

Gracie no doubt played a huge part in the success of our pack therapy theory. More than any other animal we have ever known, she instinctively knew when a new dog was scared or when an old dog was fragile. Perhaps her greatest achievement involved her work with Xera. Xera's success helped us place several other special-needs dogs in permanent homes.

We loved on Gracie for six years while she loved on the most tender of our rescues. Sadly, we lost Gracie in her eleventh year. Her cancer returned and spread rapidly. While we knew that a spirit like hers might never again grace our sanctuary, her legacy lived on in the lives of the dogs that she cared for, until they could make it on their own.

An Athlete

Opal Ann was a double dapple. She did not suffer the usual physical disabilities that often come with the unique coloring. Opal Ann enjoyed complete function in her eyes and ears. Her sister, Xera Mae already lived at the sanctuary when Opal Ann's owners decided to give her up. They seemed to know each other even though they had been separated for over a year. They played and fought together like sisters.

Tiny, but muscular, Opal Ann could have been a track star. She displayed one of the highest activity levels we had seen in a Dachshund. Opal Ann only had one passion: chasing a ball. She chased a tennis ball as long as we could force ourselves to throw it. When we had our fundraiser, she succeeded in getting quite a few of the guests to throw a ball for her. Some threw it, I think, as a way to get the wet tennis ball off their laps rather than as entertainment for Opal Ann, but she did not concern herself with those obvious personal problems.

She too was Rick's dog. She waited with baited breath for him to come into the house at night so he could throw her ball. And once the games began, she did not leave him alone for hours. They both took pride in her ability to catch the ball on the rebound, and heaven forbid one of the other dogs got in her way or acted like he wanted the ball. Her tolerance level for any type of interference was negligible.

I remember one week when Rick worked even longer hours than usual, he could barely get through his dinner before he collapsed on the bed. Opal Ann rushed to his side, wagging her tail, anxious for her game of fetch. He tried his best to satisfy her. He threw the ball as fast as he could, over and over, for about twenty minutes. But his exhaustion took over. He laid his head back on his pillow and fell asleep. Not at all deterred by his lack of enthusiasm, Opal Ann placed the ball on his lap. When he did not respond, she picked it up and dropped it on his lap again. She tried that technique several times and could not get him to respond. I picked up the ball and threw it for her. She retrieved it and put it back on Rick's lap. I told her no and to leave him alone. Opal Ann looked at me with stubborn eyes that said, "Dear woman, you do not have a say in this activity, so kindly stay out of it!" So I got the ball and put it away.

What I did not know was that Opal Ann had her own stash of balls. Almost immediately, she stood back at Rick's side with another ball in her mouth. A new strategy deemed necessary at this point, prompting her to crawl up on his pillow. From that vantage point, Opal Ann dropped the ball over his shoulder; it rested on his chest just above his folded arms. When he didn't wake up, she tried to reach down from her perch on his shoulder to retrieve the ball, but she slipped and ended up on top of the ball on Rick's chest. This, of course, woke him up, and he automatically threw the ball for her again. Our little athlete was not going to be denied her nightly workout!

Anyone that has ever loved a Dachshund knows that they tend to have bad teeth. Opal Ann was no exception to that rule. At only seven years old, she suffered a reaction to anesthesia during a routine dental cleaning. We lost our little athlete quite suddenly that day, and the blow was devastating. The pain lingers to this day in Rick's heart. He knew they should have had many more years of playing fetch ahead of them. He buried her, wrapped in a favorite blanket, with her ball by her side.

A Miner

Charlie, already twelve years old when he came to our sanctuary, could best be described as lean and strong. We never knew why his previous owners turned him over to rescue. We fell in love with his little gray face instantly. Charlie's activity level surpassed all the other seniors in our care. He seldom napped in the sunshine, and never participated in the pool activities or the wrestling matches among the younger dogs.

Instead, Charlie spent his time digging in my flower bed. Actually, it could hardly be called a flower bed with one huge crepe myrtle and an old rose bush that only bloomed every other year. But for whatever reason, Charlie picked the corner of that space to dig. We often teased that someday Charlie could dig through to China, and we would have a completely different situation on our hands. Rick and I tried for months to get him to stop digging. We filled his hole every few days, only to find the excavation had begun anew the next day. We even tried filling it up with water. That didn't stop Charlie. We found him neck deep in the water, trying to figure out how to dig through the mud. One day, I went out to find Charlie at feeding time. His hole had gotten so deep, I couldn't even see the top of his head over the railroad tie that served as the flower bed border. Charlie was a miner on a mission.

During the summer of 2004, we held a fund-raiser here at the sanctuary. The house and yard overflowed with people. Most of our pack ran around from one person's leg to another gathering up all the praise and petting they could get: but not Charlie. He had a schedule to keep and nothing could deter that work. He spent the entire afternoon excavating with no regard for the high activity and noise level around him.

Most of our dogs favored me or they favored Rick. Charlie definitely favored Rick. Every evening when Rick came home, Charlie ran to his hole to show off his progress. He would dig for a minute, and then look up at Rick for a nod of approval. Even when Charlie approached the end of his time with us, he still went to his little private mine whenever Rick came home. Obviously proud of his progress, Charlie never realized that we prayed for him to change his profession.

Charlie was fourteen years old and still digging every day, when his little body finally succumbed to a bad heart. His dedication to his excavation will forever linger in our memories, and we found it fitting to make that spot his final resting place.

Chapter 4
Senior Moments

A lot can be learned from sitting down and listening to old folks. The same can be said about watching old dogs. Many distinguished, elderly Dachshunds have passed through our sanctuary over the years. Quite a few came to us after they reached their senior years, and some grew old with us. No matter how long these white faced, slow-moving dogs spent with us, we learned something of great value from each of them. I've mentioned that the dogs we rescued taught us everything we needed to know to care for them; the old dogs we rescued taught us so much more.

Old Women

Liza Jane, at the age of thirteen, lost the only home she had ever known because she snapped at a toddler. All of us over the age of fifty experience aches and pains that make us sore and grumpy. Liza Jane, at twenty-two pounds on a small frame, obviously suffered from arthritis. We suspected all along that her pain caused her to lash out at a rambunctious child. She grieved the loss of that family for months after she joined us, while we worked hard to get her down to a more manageable weight.

With some pain meds and the loss of a few pounds, Liza's zest for life improved. She became our hall monitor. When the dogs' play escalated to the point that she felt they might lose control, Liza Jane placed her body in their path and howled. Many times she distracted the grappling youngsters just long enough to calm them down a bit. She never once snapped at any of the other dogs, and they offered her the same respect. She taught us the power of wisdom.

Entirely too many seniors came from homes where they had spent their entire lives. Poco came to us in her twelfth year. Her previous owner explained that she was taking a new job that would keep her away from home too much to care for Poco. She enjoyed two more years here with us. April ended up in a shelter in Richardson at the estimated age of fifteen. Her history remained a mystery, but the giant cyst on the side of

her face gave us a clue. Doc Jess drained the cyst, and April survived a few more months with us. Gertie came from another owner, too busy to be inconvenienced by her pet's advanced age and ever increasing needs. She had lived ten years in the same home. These old girls taught us the essence of forgiveness.

Sugar's estimated age of twelve showed in her silver face. The joints in her back legs had frozen stiff with arthritis, but Sugar never showed any sign of being in pain. She always stood beside me while I worked in the kitchen, rubbing her head against my legs. Sugar became one of my shadows. I learned quickly to check around me before taking a step because she would invariably be standing close enough to trip me if I moved. Out in the yard she followed every step I took. If I stopped walking, she stopped walking. If I got up on the porch, she got up on the porch. I knew every time I felt a dog rubbing my leg, I would find Sugar right there beside me. She taught us the gratification of devotion.

At the age of fourteen Mitzi's lifelong owner passed away. Gray hair consumed her entire body except for one little patch of red at the end of her tail. Mitzi's anguish enveloped her like a dark, looming storm. Occasionally, she cried out in her sleep; a low, whimpering sound that no doubt came from her broken heart. Mitzi only lived three weeks after arriving at the sanctuary. We did what we could to comfort her, and the old ladies accepted her into their group, but nothing could replace the hole in her heart. She taught us that grief can, occasionally, be fatal.

Christy Vaughn Eicher, V spent her entire nineteen years with us. She enjoyed an enchanted life: healthy food, lots of exercise, regular vet care, mountains of praise, and oceans of love. Christy reigned over our home like a queen until a brain tumor took her from us. She lived long enough to watch our budding rescue efforts begin to bloom. Christy taught us the legacy of love.

Ida Mae's estimated age when we first saw her was thirteen. Her almost black teeth smelled so badly I had to roll down the windows in the car on the way home from the shelter. Her hair fell out when I touched her, and her ears oozed from infection. After a few weeks of antibiotics, she lost the last of her teeth in her dental surgery. We used therapeutic baths and lotions to fight the skin problems. Ida Mae lived another two years here at the sanctuary. She taught us to admire perseverance.

We were lucky enough to rescue several old females from puppy mills. Cheyenne was one of the first. She had several big mammary tumors. Her surgery was successful and she recovered completely within a few weeks. She enjoyed the yard and spent most of her time napping in a favorite spot under one of the large pecan trees. Cheyenne cuddled with the old women on the back porch, and Rick teased that she had actually been the founding member of the local "Red Hat Society." Heidi Louise came to us at the age of eleven from a puppy mill. She still carried milk in her bags; proof that she had recently given birth. After a dangerously long surgery to spay her, Heidi 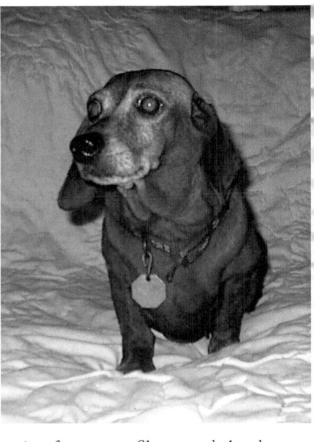 Louise recovered with the voracity of a teenager. She ran and played in the yard with an energy level that put some of our younger dogs to shame. Zoe also came from a puppy mill. She spent the first nine years of her life living on wire. She had never walked on grass before, and Rick and I both cried the first time she did. These sweet ladies taught us the value of resilience.

Maxine, Prissy, Cori, Luci, Trish, Bella, Margo, Amy, Duchess, Cricket, Ginger, Emmy Lou, Ariel, Dee Dee, Penny, Sunshine, and Minnie also came through our sanctuary as old, un-adoptable females.

Old Men

Certainly, we learned many of the same lessons from the vintage males in our care. But when I think back over the years and read my journals, many of the stories that come to mind about the old boys, make me laugh. Over the years we have rescued and cared for more old females than old males. One of the reasons for that statistic is that the males in puppy mills do not live to be old. Another reason for the larger numbers of female dogs is that male dogs don't get adopted out of the shelters nearly as often. They are seen as more trouble to train and more likely to cause problems, and therefore they are more likely to be euthanized. We feel very lucky to have been able to save as many old men as we did, and most of them proved to be extremely entertaining.

Found wondering a secluded oil field road, Dudley became our first senior rescue. His estimated age of twelve was evident in his graying face and the scarce amount of teeth in his mouth. We had only rescued one

other dog, André when we received Dudley. So the two of them and our own three dogs made up the entire pack. Dudley had just settled in when we acquired four other dogs in two days time. Nearly doubled in size, our pack dynamic began to evolve quickly. The Rat Pack formed their own little club. They played rather voraciously, and soon it became apparent that Dudley often disapproved. He would rush forward during a wrestling match and bump chests with the involved males. We nicknamed him Deputy Dudley; he just wanted to keep the peace. By the end of August 2001, our pack had increased to thirteen dogs. Dudley's duties as deputy multiplied, and he took them very seriously.

Rickashay came to us in October 2001. He was estimated to be fourteen years old and was completely toothless. Being almost paralyzed in his back legs did not stop him from getting almost everywhere he wanted to go. Rickashay barked constantly. He raised his head to the sky when he barked, and he used that motion to help move himself forward. While he could walk a little, most of the time he bounced forward in conjunction with each bark, so we nicknamed him Rickashay Rabbit. He apparently had a streak of vanity because I often found him admiring himself in the mirror. *Looking good!* Five times during the fourteen months that Rickashay spent at the sanctuary, he experienced a severe seizure. Each time he quit barking for several days. Before the first seizure, I might have paid Rickashay to stop barking for a few days, but when he did stop barking after each seizure, I prayed to hear that bark again.

JR came to us as a hero. He had stopped an intruder from breaking into his owner's apartment in Houston by barking and raising a ruckus. His picture appeared in the local newspaper, and his owner loved him very much. Unfortunately for JR and his owner, Ashley, a drastic change in her life made it impossible for them to stay together. Ashley

searched for a special place for her little guy and was thrilled when she found the sanctuary. She drove him to us and visited with the other dogs for awhile before her teary-eyed departure.

JR, the epitome of a gentleman, loved everyone, human and canine, alike. He needed to lose a bit of weight, and he did so very quickly. JR developed a habit shortly after his arrival that to this day has us puzzled. He walked up to my crepe myrtle and rested his head on the lower branches, and then just sat down. Sometimes he sat there for thirty minutes or more. Rick and I first thought he might be watching the sparrows that nested in that bush, but he never moved when they flew. He continued that strange maneuver even during the winter, when the bush had no leaves and no birds. *Whatcha doing, big guy?*

Luke was another big dachshund. Like so many of the seniors we received as owner turn-ins, Luke needed to lose a bit of weight. Once that happened, his achy back improved, and he enjoyed an active life. Luke ran and played quite a bit with the Rat Pack, and we were surprised at how well an eight year-old could keep up with the youngsters. Luke, however, had a favorite pastime that did not make our other dogs happy. He walked through the yard seeking out sleeping dogs. Once he found someone sound asleep and not paying him any attention, he walked past him two or three times. Then, from about two feet away, he turned his back on them and started backing up until he could sit down on the sleeping dog. He appeared to have found the perfect perch for about five seconds, until the sleeping dog wiggled out from under him and walked away miffed. When Luke's bottom hit the ground, he'd stand up, and search the yard again for a new unsuspecting comfy chair.

Teddy, Rusty, Colonel, Lucky, Caleb, Charlie, Rascal, Hans, Pepe, Barnie, Willie, Duke, Moses, Jefferson, Colton, Fritz, and Schultz all came to us in their senior years. Some lived with us for several years, some only a few days. We made sure that every day at the sanctuary was the best day we could give these old timers.

Old dogs lose their value in our society. Over the years, Rick and I have suffered the loss of many dogs. Our hearts break each time Rick is forced to add another grave to our ever expanding cemetery. But the lessons we learned from each and every one of their precious little hearts kept us going. Wisdom, forgiveness, devotion, love, perseverance, resilience, humor, and even grief, are all elements in our ability to continue to follow our destiny.

I wish everyone that walks through a local shelter looking for the perfect, young female dog could spend a few days here watching our pack. The lessons learned and the characters discovered behind so many gray faces might surprise many people. Old dogs are not a perfect fit for every family. However, old dogs bring enough love to fill many homes; old dogs bring enough wisdom to teach everyone something; old dogs can have funny, wonderful personalities; and old dogs have value.

Chapter 5
Special Lives

Special-needs dogs fall into one of two categories: they are either born with special-needs, or life has made them that way. Most of the disabilities we have dealt with are physical, but a few of our little ones have had psychological problems. No matter the nature of the infirmity, we used all the tools at our disposal to come up with a plan for their care. Those plans ranged from extremely simple, to exhaustingly complex schemes. Doc Jess was the major player in the plans that involved illness and injury. Rick worked to deal with the psychological puzzles. My job was to implement these plans and come up with innovative ways to accommodate the situations that could not be fixed with medication, surgery, or behavioral therapy.

Born That Way

Piccolo came to us at only six weeks of age in the summer of 2004. She could not walk or stand. Doc Jess took one look at her and said, "She has frog legs". She explained that Piccolo's joints and tendons had some weaknesses that prevented her from standing. Piccolo needed extensive physical therapy, but her chances of growing up without a noticeable disability were excellent. Our niece Jordon worked for us that summer. Upon arriving home with Piccolo, I found Jordon in the wading pool with Xera. I approached the pool with that adorable little puppy, and Jordon squealed with delight. I explained the situation to her and told her that if she was willing to do the therapy, that Piccolo could be hers. Each day after that, Jordon worked with Piccolo's legs. Before too many days passed, Piccolo could already stand, and soon after that she tried to walk. Day after day, Jordon put her in the pool and worked with those legs. She ate her lunch with Piccolo in her lap and worked those legs. Eventually they took daily walks. Within two months, Piccolo could walk just like a normal, clumsy puppy. Such an easy fix for such a special life.

Brachygnathism Malocclusion! *Say what?* That is the medical term for parrot mouth, and Phoenix had a severe case. Rescued off the streets, he faced the very real possibility of starving to death. Phoenix's lower jaw was a full three inches shorter than his upper jaw. In fact his lower jaw barely existed and contained no teeth. We could not figure out how he had survived to be nearly a year old. Phoenix could not have nursed from his mom; someone had to have fed him with a dropper or a bottle as a puppy. How he went from that kind of special care to being on the streets remains an unsolved puzzle.

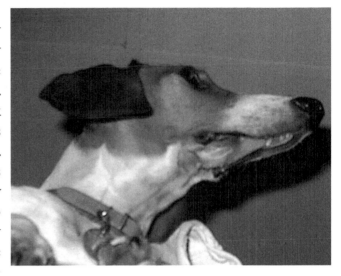

Phoenix's upper jaw was too long to allow him to scoop or bite food with his lower jaw. He could barely drink without submerging his nose in a bowl of water. No surgical solutions existed to fix his severely deformed mouth, so practical ways to allow Phoenix to eat became my number one challenge. I tried flat plates. I tried several shapes of bowls. I tried wet food. I tried dry food. Several things worked slightly, but nothing worked to give him the ability to eat the way he needed. Although I managed to get some food in him every day, he did not gain an ounce.

However, like most disabled animals, Phoenix learned to adapt. He maneuvered his upper snout just to the outside of our water dishes, which allowed him to scoop water with his tongue. That tactic became my focus. I worked out the logistics of a food dish that allowed him to eat more food before his frustration caused him to give up. I finally settled on a small flat plate with a raised rim.

Rick built a stand that held this plate in place and up to the level of Phoenix's jaw. This allowed him to eat quicker and to get more of the food into his mouth. The rim on the plate allowed me to fill it with enough food to satisfy his needs. Phoenix learned to eat the same way he drank, with his tongue. He scooped the food up over the rim where it fell into his tiny lower jaw. It took him a bit longer to eat than the other dogs, but he began to eat full portions. I didn't worry about his inability to chew. Dachshunds rarely chew their food; they just suck it down.

Phoenix, a brown and white piebald, loved everyone. He loved to run and play and became an integral part of the wrestling matches in the yard. Quite often, Phoenix was the last man standing, ready to play when the others tired of the game and found a place to nap. He filled out, and his coat gained a shiny gloss after only a few weeks with his new eating stand. Phoenix's ability to adjust was remarkable, and he reaped the benefits throughout his life.

Double Dapples

Xera, Opal Ann, Jefferson, Mariah, Patch, Taffy, Cricket, Hannah, Kathy Jane, Benjamin and Zachariah were all double dapples. With the exceptions of Opal Ann and Cricket, all of these dogs came into this world with hearing and/or sight disabilities that directly resulted from less than desirable breeding techniques. The luckiest of those dogs ended up with a rescue group.

Opal Ann and Xera came from the same litter of four. Three of those dogs were born deaf and blind. Why Opal Ann got lucky, we don't know, but one out of four is not good odds. We have cared for eleven double dapples here at the sanctuary, and only two enjoyed completely healthy sight and hearing.

Dealing with a blind dog has always been difficult, most especially when they are introduced to a new environment. Dealing with a deaf dog was a bit easier, but still challenging. Dealing with a blind and deaf dog presented a monumental task. Xera was our first double dapple and teaching her how to live happily among our pack helped prepare us for the others. The chronicle of Xera's success on our website encouraged prospective adoptive families to consider Mariah, Hannah, Benjamin, and Zachariah. These four double dapples came to us as young dogs. All were blessed with some ability to hear, but they all suffered from a high degree of blindness. Placing these precious little dogs who happened to be blind, or nearly blind, felt like a miracle to us. They all lived happy, long lives in their new homes. Very special lives, at that.

Taffy, Patch, and Kathy Jane all came to the sanctuary as six week old puppies. Taffy lived a long, happy life here, and Patch remains a member of our pack, having just celebrated her fourteenth birthday. Kathy Jane was born blind and partially deaf. On top of those afflictions, she had fluid on her brain. Her extremely swollen head made it difficult for her to balance so she couldn't stand up on her own. Doc Jess told us her condition was rare and little could be done about it, but we could try. She prescribed a steroid in an attempt to eliminate some of the fluid in Kathy Jane's head. The meds hadn't had enough time to take effect when we found her lifeless body. We didn't get to love her for very long, but for those two days her puppy breath, her sweet little feet, and her delight at receiving our love made her short life very special.

Life Dishes It Out

Dogs fall prey to many different types of injuries, from many different types of situations. Most of us do everything in our power to protect our little furry children. But accidents happen. And, as distressing as it can be to hear, a few of us are capable of cruelty. Our sanctuary has housed many wounded dogs over the years, with varying degrees of severity. As with the dogs that come to us with illnesses or genetic malfunctions, the dogs that came to us hurt or recovering have a resilience that most humans can not imagine.

Levi initiated us in the rescue of wounded dogs. I found him on a local shelter's website. His right eye had swelled to twice it's normal size; he had been hit by a car. Levi was tall for a Dachshund and skinny. His rough coat almost glowed orange — the strangest color on a Dachshund I had ever seen. Levi's bones protruded under his skin, and blood caked his tail and the side of his head. His tail had been severed. Part of it dangled from a thin strip of skin to lay flat on the ground.

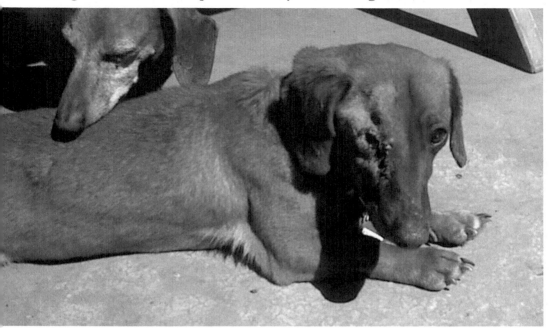

I called Doc Jess and drove straight to the clinic. After examining this surprisingly calm dog, she suggested I leave him. She gave him an IV of fluids, antibiotics, and pain meds through the night. Early the next morning, Levi went into surgery. The clinic called at noon with the news that Levi had done fine in surgery and would be awake enough to come home that afternoon. His eye had been removed, and he lost most of his tail. We never knew for sure how old this pumpkin colored fellow might be, but Levi recovered like a young dog.

After two weeks of recovering in isolation, Levi joined the pack. They all took turns sniffing him up, down, and all over. He stood perfectly still and allowed everyone their opportunity to check him out. By the next afternoon, he ran and wrestled with the Rat Pack. He had energy to spare on his new diet. Levi gained weight, and his hair grew softer to the touch, but forever remained bright orange.

Levi would not have been called mysterious in any way but one. Late each afternoon, around four o'clock, he made his way to the east end of the yard. He chose a particular spot that suited his needs. From there he could see clearly to the north for miles. Levi pulled his head up to the sky and howled like a coyote for about five minutes. This chore completed, he made his way to the porch for a nice early evening nap. The first twenty or thirty times he did that, the other dogs ran to his side and barked with him. Eventually they gave up on Levi's unseen threat and ignored him. Levi did not care. He knew something in the north sky deserved to be barked at, scared away, or told off. And Levi was the special man for the job.

Amber came to us as another victim of a lost battle with a car. She lost both eyes and part of her left ear. Her entire left side suffered tissue damage, and she always favored her front left leg. Her physical injuries had long since healed when we found her in a local Humane Society kennel, and it didn't take long for us to guess how she had acquired her wounds: she would run full force into a tree, or the fence, or another dog. Amber did not have a slow gear; everything with her happened at high speed.

Liza Jane and Gracie stayed busy trying to keep this little speedster out of trouble. Thankfully, Amber finally learned the lay of the yard. She knew where the trees stood, and she knew where the porch and the fence were. If she could just figure out how to keep the other dogs from moving around, she would be set. Rick and I knew she was special; the dogs were not so sure.

Most Accidents Happen At Home

Amy injured her right foreleg in a recliner accident. She was definitely in the wrong place at the wrong time when her owner sat up quickly in his recliner, and the foot stool injured her leg. Because of Amy's advanced age of twelve, her lifelong owner felt it best to have her put down. I was in the right place at the right time when he delivered her to the shelter. I overheard his conversation with the shelter employees and convinced them all to let me have her.

Doc Jess was forced to remove the entire leg, and Amy's recovery progressed slowly. Her physical wounds finally, after five weeks in a play pen in the dining room, healed. Emotionally, she never really gained a lot of ground. Her one joy was Rick. She loved him and responded to his voice with a quick swish of her tail.

Summer was in full swing, and that meant a lot of tractor work for Rick. He decided one afternoon to fashion a wooden box on his tractor for Amy. She had a harness to keep her safe and a cushion to lay on. The first time I watched Rick drive that tractor across our property, with Amy secure in her little box in front of him, was unforgettable. The way she perked up every time she heard that tractor fire up, knowing Rick would soon come and scoop her up for a ride, was beyond special.

Over the years we cared for dogs that incurred injuries from garage doors, dropped boxes, tripping owners, and falling tree branches. Their recoveries varied as much as their background stories. All of these little furry babies brought joy to our lives in one way or another. We felt blessed with the experience of sharing their incredible lives.

Canine Assault

Rick and I have lived in the middle of a pack of dogs for fifteen years. We are well aware and always watchful for any signs of aggression among our dogs. There have been some scuffles. There have also been a few occasions where younger more active dogs have been shifted to a different area of our sanctuary, or to another rescuer, to protect our frail seniors or special-needs residents. We still experience shock, however, when confronted with some of the damage dogs can inflict on each other.

Our weather had turned bitterly cold in February of 2005 when I received a phone call from one of our foster homes in town. They had heard a small dog barking through the night, and early the next morning they found a tiny Dachshund locked in a backyard of a vacant house. Scarlett, emaciated and still shivering, was delivered to our door within an hour. She didn't have any open wounds, but her head carried a huge scar and part of her left ear was gone. Her engorged bags proved that she had recently delivered a litter.

I immediately added a heating pad to the blanket her rescuers had her wrapped in and fixed her a bowl of hot food. Soon enough her shivering stopped, and she cleaned up that bowl in mere seconds. It wasn't until the next day at the vet clinic that we learned more about this little girl's tragic beginnings. Doc Jess recognized this dog as one of her past patients. She had seen Scarlett the first day of her life to stitch her lesions. The owners explained that Scarlett's mother had jumped on her shortly after giving birth. They rescued the puppy from her mom and took her to the clinic. We never knew if they bottle fed Scarlett or if her mom had accepted her back into her litter, but somehow she managed to make it to adulthood. And for unexplainable and inexcusable reasons, Scarlett found herself abandoned to fend for herself in deplorable conditions.

We had never heard of a mother dog attacking her babies until Scarlett came into our lives, and no one has been able to explain this behavior to us. We felt sure that Scarlett would also have emotional scars, but that could not have been further from reality.

Scarlett's personality popped out right away, and she inspired us with her will to be happy. She wagged her tail, which wagged her bottom, constantly. She had a silly smile and bright eyes that proved she held no grudges against humans. Scarlett loved to play, and she loved to be cuddled. We accommodated her need for attention for six months until we found her the perfect home. Scarlett's life had obviously been extraordinary, and she taught us that forgiveness is possible in impossible situations.

Gabriella's story is the worst case of canine aggression we have ever dealt with, and it produced images in my mind that frightened me. She had been attacked by two dogs. She lost both back legs, her entire tail, part of her nose and face, and one eye. Gabriella was taken to an emer-

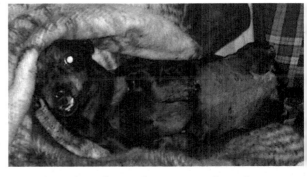

gency vet clinic in Houston by the animal control officers that responded to the call about the dog fight. That she even survived, is a testament to the excellent emergency care she received. Several weeks passed before they felt Gabriella might be well enough to leave the clinic, but no owner came forward to claim her. One of my rescue friends worked at the clinic that saved her life, so we got the call.

Rick's sister, Paula, was visiting friends in Houston at the time, and she agreed to transport Gabriella back to West Texas. She called me on the drive home, and I could tell her heart broke the minute she laid eyes on Gabriella. We had never turned down a dog in dire need of our sanctuary, but I questioned the wisdom of keeping this little girl alive. When Rick and I discussed Gabriella's situation the very first time, he said the vet clinic kept her going for so long with little chance of reimbursement, and we owed them the respect to try and care for this little survivor.

So I prepared her place. She would be in the play pen in the dining room that had recently been vacated when we sadly lost Amy. Houston is a ten hour drive from us, and it was early evening before Paula arrived with Gabriella. I knew her wounds had mostly healed, but as I reached in to get her out of the car, my hands shook; I could not bear the thought of hurting her. To my surprise, she used her back and hip muscles to move toward my hands. Once I cradled her in my arms, she melted into me as we made our way into the house. By the time I reached the dining room, Gabriella started licking my face.

I placed our newest pack member on the blankets. She scooted around a bit, turned toward me, and I could have sworn that she winked at me with her one remaining eye. While I am aware that was impossible, I later learned it would have fit her personality perfectly!

Early evening was a busy time at the sanctuary; meals and meds needed

to be given out. Rick came home shortly after I began to feed the pack and actually crawled into the play pen with Gabriella. She scooted right up to him, and he picked her up. She poured out the affection. At that moment she became Gabby, and Rick and I were crazy in love. Gabby wagged her entire bottom as she relaxed into Rick's chest. She licked his face and nuzzled her head up close to his neck. This little gal was a love bunny. I worried about her quality of life and everyone's decision to keep her alive right up until that moment.

Gabby learned our routine very quickly. Able to eat with no problem, her extra needs were minimal. I carried her outside several times each day, and she scooted around in the yard. The rest of the pack accepted her quickly, and many of them became the recipients of her affection. Gabby barked and bounced when the young dogs ran and wrestled. She became a regular cheering section for the daily events. She snuggled up to already sleeping dogs and allowed all comers to cuddle with her.

Any feelings of pity that Rick and I might have had for Gabby in the beginning evaporated in those first few days. Without realizing it, I quit seeing what was missing on Gabby; instead I saw what she still had. The traumatic events of her life melted away in our minds, because they were never apparent in her mind. Any creature that gushes love on such a grand scale had every reason to live. Gabby taught us that disabled does not equal broken.

Human Brutality

Dachshunds bark. Let me say that again for emphasis. Dachshunds bark! Some are more persistent than others, and a few probably need medical intervention to calm themselves. Shelby, most likely needed some medical help. Unfortunately, Shelby's original owners did not fully understand his needs before they took this beautiful, long-hair, miniature Dachshund into their home. At a little over a year old, Shelby had a pipe shoved down his throat in an effort to debark him. He ended up with a broken jaw.

There is some controversy about the debarking process when performed by a trained, licensed veterinarian; some call it cruelty, while others believe it saves their dogs from being labeled a nuisance. Debarked dogs can still bark, but the volume has been turned down by removing tissue from their vocal cords. I won't argue the pros and cons about a veterinarian performing a procedure that has been deemed in a dog's best interest. *I will argue the savagery of what happened to Shelby.*

Shelby came to us from a rescue group in Oklahoma. His jaw had already been wired back together, and we expected him to make a full recovery. Rick and I, both horrified by Shelby's ordeal, rejoiced when he barked. We rejoiced when he made friends here at the sanctuary. And we rejoiced when we found him, what we considered, the perfect home. Obviously, his prospective adoptive family followed their hearts when they decided to give this abused dog a good home. When Shelby came back to us after only a few months in that home, I wondered if they had given enough consideration to the fact that Shelby was an excessive barker.

Living in a country community where our nearest neighbor is several acres away, barking is not an issue. Living with thirty to forty dachshunds, barking is as much a part of the landscape as the birds singing from the trees. Our dogs bark when a siren wails. Our dogs bark when a neighbor's dog barks. Our dogs bark when a group of Guinea hens wonder onto our property, and our dogs bark when they want us to know something.

Learning to interpret the meaning behind the barking took some practice. All dog owners eventually learn that with their dogs. One bark means the mailman is at the door, another bark means a sparrow landed in the yard, and yet another bark means one of the pack is in trouble. Several times over the years, our barking dogs have warned me in time to save a dog having a seizure or one that injured his back.

There are times when I wish I could flip a switch and stop all barking when the phone rings or when Rick is trying to rest after working all night. But we love our dogs, and we take the good with the bad.

Shelby lived out his life with us, and he barked quite a bit. In our environment, that barking didn't make him unusual. His complete recovery, physically and mentally, from a horrific event in his life, made him extraordinarily special.

Chapter 6

We Have Today

The hardest thing we had to learn as rescuers was that we couldn't save all the dogs that needed us. The countless hours I spent walking through shelters all across our state made this devastatingly clear. But once a dog came into our care, we would never willingly give up on him. Unfortunately, some of the dogs that came to us were already so far gone that our abilities to help them proved sorely inadequate.

Tigger

I received an email in the fall of 2001 from a local rescuer about a couple that appeared desperate to re-home their young dog. Apparently, this Dachshund did not take to house training as quickly as they had hoped. *A Dachshund not housebroken, never heard of such a thing.* Dachshund owners will understand when I say that doxies are some of the most difficult dogs to house train.

Within a few days, Tigger arrived at the sanctuary. A bit taller than most doxies, Tigger had a beautiful black and brown coat, and a funny little smile. He immediately made friends, and I felt finding him a forever home would be a breeze. We had his vet work done right away, and everything was perfect for a few more days. Then he had a Grand Mal seizure in the kitchen. Fortunately, I had experienced seizures in our dogs before, and I knew what to do. Within seconds, I had Tigger wrapped in a towel and in my lap, away from the other dogs. I held him close until his seizure subsided. Soon, he fell into a fitful sleep that lasted for several hours.

Tigger's seizure was a game changer. The next morning, our first vet prescribed anti-seizure meds. We knew he might never leave the sanctuary. Very few adoptive homes would accept a dog that suffered from seizures, or one that took daily meds. Our plans for Tigger had to be modified.

Seizures will sometimes instigate an attack from a pack of dogs. So we watched him like a hawk. Rick and I decided to set up a small pen in the den to allow Tigger a bit more freedom. He settled in quickly and continually flashed his big, brown eyes at us. A handful of our other dogs could not quell their curiosity about this new resident. Tigger responded to their constant investigations by jumping and hopping all around his pen. He desperately wanted to play, and we allowed him to run and romp in the yard as much as we could.

Moms can always tell, by the sounds in the house, if the kids are getting into something they shouldn't. That's the feeling I had when I woke one morning. I heard Tigger's wire pen scraping across the tile floor, and I knew something was up. I went into the den to check out the commotion and Tigger was seizing. Several of the other dogs whined and scratched at the pen. I swooped them up with both hands, placed them outside, and dressed in a hurry. Within minutes, I stood in the waiting room of the vet clinic. Tigger was still in the grips of a horrible seizure when the vet tech took him from me. I resisted a bit as I did not want to leave him. She insisted that he would receive the best treatment available, and we might all be better off if I waited for news by the phone.

Regrettably, the efforts to stop Tigger's seizure failed. He seized for four hours. The receptionist called and told me the vet recommended that we euthanize him right away. I consented, and rushed to the clinic. Tigger had already been put down. Anger and frustration took hold of me, and I must admit, I made a bit of a scene in that waiting room. *I wanted to be there with him in his final moments, so he knew he was loved.* That evening, Rick buried Tigger, wrapped in his new blanket, on the land that had been his true home for less than two weeks.

I could not help but think that our efforts on Tigger's behalf fell short of our standard. Then, I realized how little control we actually had over Tigger's life and death. Our guidelines of care had precious little time to impact that sweet little dog. One thing I knew for sure: our standard for vet care had forever changed. I would never walk into that vet clinic again. That proved to be Tigger's gift to our sanctuary. I soon found Doc Jess, and everything about our interactions with our most important support system transformed permanently.

Gabbie

Gabbie (not to be confused with Gabby) came into our lives much too late. One rainy Sunday morning, I received a call from a couple that had a sick Dachshund. They did not feel they could care for her. Gabbie was only two years old, and they had no clue what was wrong with her. I agreed to meet them in a little town about fifty miles from our sanctuary. When I arrived in the designated meeting place, I spotted their car right away. The rain was pouring down, and when I pulled up beside them I could see two young girls in the back seat of the car holding a beautiful red Dachshund. The parents stepped out into the rain to greet me. They gave me a brief history of Gabbie, explaining that they acquired her as a puppy, and that she had received basic vet care. I assured them we would do our best for this little girl.

The father opened up the back door of their vehicle, and the girls inside cried, "No Daddy! Please don't Daddy!" My heart jumped up into my throat. I had not faced this situation before, and luckily for me, it never happened just that way again. This man, obviously not blessed with an overabundance of patience, proceeded to pull Gabbie from those two tiny sets of hands. The Mom turned her back on us, as he placed Gabbie in my arms. Skinny and weak, she could barely hold her head up. I searched in vain for the right words; nothing came to me. I tried to smile, as I wrapped that extremely ill dog in a blanket. The voices of those little girls crying, and the images of their faces looking through the back window haunted my dreams that night.

Once Gabbie and I arrived back home, I went into overdrive trying to figure out what I could do for her. Our experiences with senior dogs taught me to have baby food on hand; that was often the easiest thing to get an unwilling dog to eat. I managed to get her to eat a few bites off a spoon before she just couldn't eat anymore. Gabbie struggled to swallow, and I feared forcing her would put her in danger of aspirating the food. So she and I curled up in a chair while I used a syringe to get a tiny bit of water into her. Then she slept.

Rick and I spent the night taking turns holding her, trying to feed her, and trying to get a little water into her. The next morning seemed so very far away, but we managed the best way we could until the vet office opened. I rushed her to the clinic, and within a few minutes she was on an IV. Doc Jess told me that Gabbie's outlook wasn't good, and she wanted to do blood work right away. I would have to leave her there. Later that day, we learned that Gabbie had tick fever and anemia. She received IV antibiotics and fluids. By the next morning, she perked up a bit. When I arrived at the clinic to check on her, she could actually hold her head up a bit. Her little body finally quit trembling. Gabbie's condition remained extremely guarded.

For two days, I visited Gabbie, and held her for as long as my busy schedule would allow. But sadly, I received a call from Doc Jess the next morning; Gabbie took a turn for the worse. She passed away before I could get to the clinic that day, and that was the second time in two weeks that I had to carry a lifeless body home for burial. Doc Jess, Rick, and I all wondered if we had received this precious little heart only a few days earlier if we would have been able to save her. There is no way to know for sure. We all knew we had done our best for Gabbie, and we knew that in our care for those few short days she was loved.

Moses

The heartbreak of walking through countless shelters and looking into the eyes of countless dogs is almost indescribable. Some eyes begged for love and attention, some almost glazed over with fear and/or aggression, while some diverted their gaze, in faultless shame. Knowing we couldn't save them all only added to the emergent feeling to do more.

A few summers ago, I received a call from a local animal activist that convinced me to meet her at the animal shelter. This particular department of our local sheriff's office had been under siege for their inability to make progress toward a no-kill shelter. Weekly protests outside their building convinced them to give the local rescuers increased access to all the animals in their care. The public part of our local animal control building always upset me. But nothing compared to the side building where they housed the un-adoptable dogs. This is where you found the injured, the extremely ill, and the uncontrollable dogs.

My first venture into that side building had a crushing effect on me. My target, a large male dachshund, made my heart stop. He lay on his side with several immense tumors on his stomach and chest. Emaciated and weak, Moses managed a tiny wag of his tail as I entered his kennel. He could not raise his head, but his eyes met mine, and I promised him I would not let his life end there, on that cold concrete floor. I rushed toward the shelter office to fill out the paperwork and pay the fees to get him out of there. My friend asked me to stop for a second and take a look at another dog that had no chance at a new home. This one was a small bird dog mix with a front leg hanging, obviously badly broken.

I agreed very quickly to take her with me. I didn't feel that Moses had enough time for me to contemplate this other dog, much less call and discuss her with Rick.

In very short order, I had both dogs loaded in my car. I called Doc Jess on my way to her clinic, and she prepared for our arrival. The vet techs met me at the door and took Moses from my arms. By the time I got Delilah (the bird dog) out of the car and inside, Moses had an IV drip and one of the vet techs drew a blood sample. We placed Delilah in a nearby kennel, and I stood back and watched as Doc Jess examined Moses. Again, he managed to wag his tail ever so slightly and I noticed the catch in Doc Jess' voice as she gave orders to her staff. Delilah was quickly whisked away for an X-ray, while I waited for Doc Jess to look up from Moses. When she did, I could tell by her face that she did not hold much hope for him.

Later that day, I learned that Moses had diabetes and the tumors had burst and bled. Delilah's X-rays showed her mangled, front leg had to be removed; the bones were crushed, and the severe nerve damage would not allow it to heal properly. Rick and I spent the evening talking and worrying about Moses and Delilah. We both had a good idea what the next day might bring.

When the phone rang early the next morning, I dreaded the news. Moses passed away during the night. I hated that I had not been there to hold him while he died, but I loved the fact that he was wrapped in a beautiful blanket (made by Gaye) from the sanctuary when he lost the fight. The news on Delilah was much more promising. She would soon be headed for surgery, and her prognosis was good.

Young, and extremely athletic, Delilah has become a beloved member of our pack. She runs faster, jumps higher, and plays more than most of our current residents. When I look at Delilah, I know that she lives because of Moses, and I am reminded that God has a plan for each of his creatures.

Chapter 7

Two by Two

Several times over the years we rescued dogs in pairs. These dogs loved each other before they loved us, so we make it our policy to keep them together. Over the years, we have been called foolish because we believed in our dogs' devotion to each other. People told us that we couldn't give dogs human emotions; dogs don't love and grieve for each other like we do. *Not true! Not true at all.*

Eddie and Freddie

It amazed us how quickly the news of our rescue and sanctuary spread. Within a few weeks of our first official rescue in the summer of 2001, we received a call from a man in a nearby town. He had picked up two male Dachshunds running on the loop around town. He could not keep them, did not want to take them to the shelter, and certainly did not want them to remain on the streets. He received our number from a friend who got it from another friend. Though we had not established a presence online yet, the grapevine worked almost as well.

By the next afternoon, Eddie and Freddie joined us at the sanctuary. Eddie, a black and tan wiry looking guy, wasted no time exploring and running through the yard. Freddie, a red, standard, with a laid back demeanor, was more interested in enjoying my lap. He captured our hearts with his

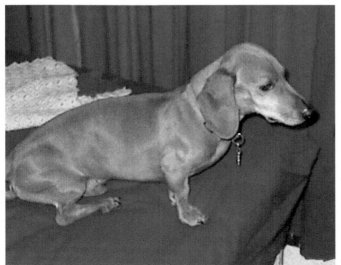

huge brown eyes. Both dogs appeared well fed, free from pests, and extremely healthy. Unfortunately, neither wore a collar. Within a few days, I posted pictures of them in several vet clinics near where they were found and all the local shelters. After a few weeks with no responses from our posted pictures or our ads in the classifieds, we tried to find them a new home together.

Several months went by before anyone showed any interest in these dogs. Placing males always proved harder than females. Two males that needed to stay together would be almost impossible. Finally, one day we got an application for them. The home visit went well, and the references checked out. So Rick and I made plans to drive them three hundred miles to their prospective new home. The trip wore us out, but we returned home hopeful that Eddie and Freddie were safe in their forever home. That feeling only lasted five days. The new owners called and informed me they could not keep Eddie and Freddie. They felt that the boys needed more training. The following weekend, I drove back across the state and brought these two guys home for good. I took their bios off our brand new website. Rick and I decided they would remain at the sanctuary, together.

Eddie blossomed into a true acrobat. He could almost fly when he ran. He is one of the few dogs we ever cared for that loved snow. In West Texas, snow is not something we deal with often. But the first good snow storm of the following winter covered us in several inches overnight. The next day we watched in  awe as Eddie flew through the snow. Most of our dogs would not even venture off the porch. *Heaven forbid they might get their little paws wet!*

Soon Eddie and Freddie became two of the original members of what we had named our Rat Pack. They wrestled, ran, played, and wrestled some more. Several other dogs over the years attempted to join the Rat Pack, but these two along with André and Brandy always instigated the rambunctious play. All between the ages of two and five, the Rat Pack were the teenagers of our pack, and they acted like it. One day, their play escalated to the point that Eddie ran straight toward the fence, placed his feet on it as he jumped, and to his surprise and mine, ended up outside the yard. Our four foot brick fence had never been breached by a Dachshund before. I guess it scared Eddie as much as it did me; he never jumped the fence again.

Eddie and Freddie had obviously grown up together. They maintained a strong friendship over the years. Except for the time Eddie spent soaring over the yard on his own, they always seemed to keep tabs on each other.

They ate together, they romped together, and they slept together. They were total opposite personality types, but their connection was strong.

After their first year at the sanctuary, Freddie became extremely ill. He would not eat, and he would not drink. His eyes sank back into his head and overnight he appeared emaciated. Freddie was diagnosed with E-coli, and his kidneys were shutting down. He stayed at the clinic for four days on IVs. Eddie didn't play, wrestle, or run the entire time Freddie was away. But they both wagged and pranced like crazy when we brought Freddie home. *Relief!* After only a week at home, Freddie's activity level was completely back to normal. The Rat Pack, back together again, dominated the backyard fun.

Sadly, Eddie didn't live to be an old man. We lost him suddenly when he was only seven years old. We never knew why he died, as he never showed any sign of illness. We didn't have much time to grieve his loss, though, because our next problem consumed us quickly. How would Freddie deal with his loss?

For several weeks after Eddie died, Freddie searched for him. He stayed away from the pack and walked the fence line, over and over. He growled at any other dog that looked like it might lay on the blanket he and Eddie had shared. Rick and I tried to comfort Freddie, but he would not have it. He combed every inch of our property, every day. André tried to get him to wrestle; he showed no interest. So we could only watch and worry. After what seemed like an eternity, Freddie started coming back to us. Slowly, he began to take interest in the other dogs again, and at long last, he played. He did, however, continue to reserve the place beside him on his blanket, just in case Eddie came home.

Freddie lived for another five years. We estimated his age to be fifteen when he laid down on his blanket one night and died. Freddie had been with us for ten years; longer than any other rescue, with the single exception of André. We consoled ourselves with two thoughts: Freddie had a wonderful life here at the sanctuary, and he and Eddie were together again. That's what we always wanted for them.

Atticus and Abraham

These two little guys came to us from south Texas. The only true brothers we ever rescued, they looked almost identical. Atticus had a bit more dark hair on his face and ears, but other than that they were twins.

At five years old, their reason for ending up in a shelter was a mystery to us. All the data on their past could have been written on one line. We knew they had been neutered, but the owner did not give any further information, other than their ages and the fact that they came from the same litter.

Atticus might have been a few minutes older than Abraham, as he obviously made the decisions for the two of them. When it came time to eat, Abraham waited for Atticus to start before he ate. When it came time to rest, Abraham waited on Atticus to settle in on their bed, and then he joined him. When it came time to go outside, Atticus always went through the doggie door first.

They were so cute! They would walk across the room, sides touching, as if an invisible thread connected them to each other. Rick teased that they had once been conjoined twins. When they slept, Atticus always rested his head on Abraham; their two tiny bodies occupied a six inch square. If we picked one of them up, the other one stood on our shoes waiting to be reunited with his brother.

These boys did not make socializing with the other dogs a priority. They mostly stayed off to themselves, content with their own company. Patch, our pack busy-body, occasionally tried to squeeze in-between them on their bed. Atticus resisted her attempts, but eventually had to get up and move to a new blanket to avoid Patch's interference. Abraham, of course, followed Atticus every time.

Our first visit to the vet with these two caused a commotion in the waiting room. They drew attention just like identical twins. Patient and sweet, they allowed everyone to pet them as long as they continued to touch each other. I teased Doc Jess about needing to weigh them together, and dividing that number by two to arrive at an accurate weight for each dog. She drew blood, administered shots, and checked out their teeth while they stood side by side on the table.

Once the test results came in, the mood changed completely. We finally knew why they had been turned over to the shelter. Atticus tested positive for heartworms. Throughout our rescue experience, this was the only time we dealt with heartworms. We live in the desert, and heartworms are rare here. Doc Jess educated me on the treatment and care Atticus needed to survive. His infestation was severe, and his therapy would be difficult. Severe cases of heartworms are treated by injections that kill off the worms. During the three months of treatment and for the following three months, the dog must be kept as inactive as possible. Atticus' heart needed time to rid itself of the dead worms, and exercise might complicate that process.

I needed time to digest this news and talk it over with Rick. Doc Jess understood, but warned me not to take too long to decide our course of action. That evening, Rick held Atticus and Abraham while we discussed our options. We were in the middle of the summer rush season when all rescues fill up. Our sanctuary was overflowing with fifty-one dogs. I had several transports planned for the next two weeks, including a huge one to Albuquerque to take eleven adoptable dogs to meet a rescue buddy from California. Desperation set in when I heard Atticus cough for the first time. That was a sign that the worms had begun to affect his heart.

Before we could make a decision, Charlotte, my transport coordinator, called. She needed to finalize the plans for the upcoming transport to Albuquerque. She could tell by my voice that something was going on. I relayed the information of the day to her, and she immediately said, "I will take Atticus and Abraham." She lived alone and worked part time. Charlotte assured me she had already been thinking about adopting Atticus and Abraham from the moment their pictures went up on the website.

Waves of relief flooded over us as Charlotte thought out loud about how to get the boys to her, two hundred and fifty miles away. Rick and I knew that we could work out the cost of the treatment for Atticus. What we could not figure out, was how to keep him still for six months. The thought of both boys having to be in an isolation room for that length of time did not set well with either of us. Our pack's activity level had skyrocketed with the influx of summer arrivals, and we still had most of the summer ahead of us. By the time I finished my evening chores, Charlotte called back. She already had the two-part transport worked out. Dee would meet me twenty miles from the sanctuary and drive the boys to meet Dave. He was scheduled to finish the transport, and Atticus and Abraham would be at Charlotte's house by early evening the next day.

The only thing left for Rick and me to do was to convince our hearts to let these two little guys go. Of course, we knew this was the only plan that made sense; the best plan for Atticus and Abraham. By ten the next morning, I handed over two of the cutest dogs I ever met to Dee. The transport went off without a hitch, and Charlotte called me by six o'clock. She had the boys on her lap. I could hear in her voice how thrilled she was to have them in her home. We all knew Atticus and Abraham exploded the cuteness scale, and Charlotte's heart nearly burst with joy.

Atticus began his treatment for heartworms right away. Charlotte took both boys with her for each of Atticus' shots. The next six months passed very slowly for all three of them. Atticus' cough worsened as the worms inside him began to die. Charlotte worried over him like a new parent. Abraham understood that his brother did not feel well. Charlotte sent me a picture of the twins sleeping soon after Atticus' last treatment. They were snuggled up in their bed, side by side, just as they had always done at the sanctuary. This time, Abraham was the one resting his head over his brother's body protecting him the only way he knew how.

The week before Christmas, I got a call from Charlotte. She had just received the most precious gift. Atticus' little heart was clear of worms. His coughing had lessened significantly, and once again he and Abraham received the okay to play and enjoy Charlotte's beautiful backyard. Charlotte's friends and neighbors threw a "No More Worms" party. The entire neighborhood had fallen in love with those brothers, and the festivities marked the beginning of a new life for Atticus and Abraham. Charlotte's new family enjoyed three years of love.

In early January of 2008, Charlotte found Atticus lifeless in his bed with Abraham's head resting, as always, over his brother's back. The vet told her that his heart had suffered permanent damage from the heartworms, and that eventually led to his heart giving out. We all grieved over the loss of little Atticus, but Charlotte and I immediately feared the effect on Abraham. His grief took hold and robbed him of all joy. Charlotte refused to leave him alone and received the okay from her boss to bring Abraham to work with her each day. He rested on a bed on her desk, and everyone loved on him as much as they could. By spring, Abraham gradually recovered, but he never stopped yearning for his brother.

Abraham lived another four years, to the age of twelve. His little face had turned mostly gray, and his ability to hear betrayed him. One of Charlotte's neighbors buried Abraham beside his brother in the corner of the backyard. Charlotte's grief spread throughout the neighborhood, and I was thankful she had a support system to lean on. Several weeks later, those wonderful friends bought a beautiful little monument to place on Atticus' and Abraham's graves. It was engraved with their names above two tiny dogs, standing side by side.

Dee Dee and Schultz

Twice, we rescued a mother and son pair. The first such pair came to us from a vet clinic in Ft. Worth. Dee Dee, the mom, was thirteen years old and she had a very poor quality of life. A miniature, mostly gray Dachshund, Dee Dee only weighed five pounds. She literally looked like a skeleton with skin stretched over it. Shultz, her son, was a large standard. At eleven-years-old, he needed to lose at least five pounds of his twenty-three pound weight. He had just had a dental, and his overall health appeared to be good.

These two needed to be together, but not at eating time. Schultz gobbled up everything in sight that might be food. Dee Dee barely even sniffed at her food. So we put Schultz on a low calorie kibble, and we tried to get baby food down his mom. Dee Dee flat out refused to eat many days. I tried everything in my arsenal. When she turned down scrambled eggs, I almost gave up hope. Finally, I had a little luck with boiled chicken. She never ate as much as I would have liked, but she eventually gained a pound. Schultz started loosing weight right away. The high activity level in the yard insured he got plenty of exercise, and within a few months he dropped four pounds.

Dee Dee didn't venture out into the yard much. I carried her out on warm days to allow her to soak up a little sunshine, but within a few minutes she would make her way back to the porch, wanting her bed. When it came time for everyone to start bedding down at night, Schultz sought out his mom to cuddle beside her on her blanket. As soon as she felt his warm body, she crawled up on his back and slept. Rick and I had never seen anything like it. Schultz at almost four times her weight, provided a stable platform for his tiny mother to rest on. They slept that way every night for several months.

Our struggle to get Dee Dee to eat remained a challenge. She would eat one day, and not eat at all the next day. Doc Jess gave me a tube of high calorie supplement, and that helped for a few days, but then Dee Dee refused to even lick that off a spoon. Rick and I were heartsick when she became impossible to feed. Everything that had worked temporarily stopped working at all. What little quality of life she still enjoyed evaporated within a few days. I did not hesitate at that point to make the final decision to stop that little lady's suffering.

Our focus then turned to Schultz. We feared his reaction to the loss of his mom, but we wanted to give him an opportunity to say goodbye. Alone, in one of the back bedrooms of our home, we placed Dee Dee's little body on the blanket she loved. Shultz walked right up to her, sniffed her briefly, and curled up beside her. Normally, we would have buried Dee Dee in her favorite blanket, but Rick suggested that maybe Schultz needed that blanket more than she did. He slept on that blanket for another three years, until one morning when we found he had gone to be with his mom during the night.

Grief for our dogs came in as many different forms as it does for us. Some of our dogs suffered terribly after a loss, and some seemed to accept fate rather quickly. Schultz accepted the loss of his mom without any noticeable consequences. Maybe he sensed that her life had gotten too difficult to bear, maybe the many other older dogs in our care helped him accept his loss, or maybe he could still feel her laying on his back when he slept on her blanket.

Pete and Lucy

The other mother-son duo we rescued are still here with us today. These two chocolate brown Dachshunds came from a local breeder early in 2005. Pete was born missing his two back feet. The breeder told me he lost his feet during a difficult delivery but that proved to be untrue. Pete  has pads on the end of his back legs where his feet should be. That would not have happened if his disability had been caused at birth. Lucy also has genetic problems; her tail twists drastically to the left, and her head is also curved to the left. She walks sideways and resembles a backward C. Her pace is slower than most dogs, but she still gets around very well. I know nothing about genetics, but I think these two would make an interesting study. They are rare, as Dachshunds, in that they never need dental work. Pete is now twelve years old, and Lucy is fourteen; their teeth are still clean, and without decay.

Pete gets around some, but obviously won't win any races. The pads on his back legs are tender, and he prefers walking on grass or blankets. We installed concrete ramps to our back porch years ago, and Pete does not like to walk on them. Our contractor made grooves across both ramps to help some of our older dogs get traction. These grooves, apparently, are too rough for Pete's little pads. Up until a few months ago, he was able to get close to the side of the ramp, and jump up to the porch. Now, his strength is waning a bit so he barks, non-stop, when he is ready to go to bed. Many nights one of us goes outside when Pete raises a ruckus, to help him get back on the porch. Most nights this occurs at dusk, but occasionally it happens again in the middle of the night. Poor Rick doesn't sleep as soundly as I do, so the chore of getting Pete back inside in the middle of the night generally falls on him.

Our back porch has been completely enclosed. We installed a wood burning stove for heat and a window AC for the hot summers. The two ramps are placed at each end, one leads to the doggie door, and the other is outside the people door. A huge portion of this porch is covered with beds and blankets. Pete and Lucy have their favorite spot where they crawl under a blanket on one of the beds and sleep side by side.

Bonded pairs of dogs in rescue are rare. These four examples are the only bonded pairs we have received. It is wonderful to watch their devotion and love for each other, and heartbreaking to watch when one of them loses the other. More than anything else, these stories have taught us that dogs do share the same emotions we as humans experience.

Chapter 8
I Don't Want to Grow Up

During our youth, many of us have had one or two friends we felt might never really grow up: the perpetual class clowns, the party hearty types, and those that refused to accept responsibility for their actions. Rick and I have rescued a few dogs that also fit perfectly into that category. Patch and Taffy came to us as six-week-old puppies, both born with sight disabilities from their double dapple breeding, and both refused to grow up.

Patch

Early in 2002, we got a call about a puppy that had been rescued from a breeder in south Texas. With the help of our friend, Christine, Patch came to the sanctuary as an addition to a previously planned transport, and

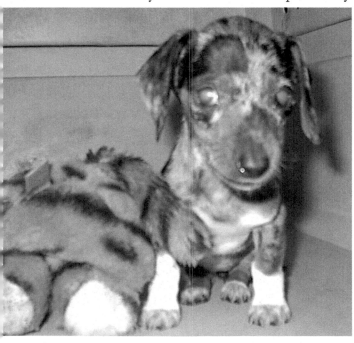

the entire world fell in love. Her coat was black, brown, gray, and white, and her huge eyes sparkled with attitude. Two days after I put her picture and story on our website, I received several applications to adopt her. Our policy, however, stood firm; no dogs left our sanctuary until they had been spayed. Patch would need to stay with us for at least three months. During that time, Patch became an integral part of our pack dynamic.

I believe that because we dealt with so many seniors and so many injured and ill dogs, that having a healthy, playful puppy around brightened not only our world, but the lives of the other dogs. Patch's eyesight, although diminished somewhat, still allowed her to navigate the sanctuary very well. She pushed and prodded her way into everyone's world. Nurse Gracie had fallen so hard for Patch that we could not stand the thought of splitting them up. By the time Patch was old enough to be spayed and had completed her series of puppy shots, we could not give her up.

This decision rattled a few cages in the rescue world. A few rescuers felt the need to scold us. One lady that sent in an application to adopt Patch became so angry with me that I finally stopped answering her daily emails. We felt the decision to keep Patch in our pack made perfect sense, and certainly it was our decision to make.

Patch was a busybody. She insisted on becoming involved in every situation. If the Rat Pack ran and played, Patch got in the way and barked. If the senior ladies decided to congregate on the porch, (*I bet they were talking about the old men.*) Patch got right in their faces and barked until they ganged up on her and ran her off the porch. If a dog found a new toy, Patch tried to steal it. One day, I watched her try to steal a new rope toy from two young males involved in a game of tug of war. When she couldn't take it away from them, she sat on it. She became everyone's annoying little sister. She even tried once to steal a water bottle from Xera. But she only tried once.

Often, Patch would run back and forth between two dogs, barking and jabbing them with her nose. She continued agitating them until they responded, with warning barks of their own. Once in awhile she kept this up until she started a scuffle. At that point, Patch bounced away as if she hadn't even been involved in their foolishness.

Bouncing is not a complete description of Patch's gait. She did bounce, but often her front end bounced in a different direction than her back end. A slinky could have replaced her mid-section, and it would not have changed the way Patch got around. She was the perfect clown, and the sanctuary provided her with the perfect stage.

Patch had another habit that eventually got her into trouble. She ate things. She ate corners off of blankets. She ate small pieces of bark. She ate pecans out of the yard. And eventually, she ate a small piece of a rubber toy, and it got stuck in her intestines. Patch became very ill, and Doc Jess had to perform emergency surgery on her to remove the toy. Within a few weeks, Patch recovered, and thankfully, she resumed her position of pack busybody.

Soon after Patch's fourth birthday, I found her in the yard, unable to stand on her back legs. X-rays showed that she had severely damaged two vertebrae in her back. Doc Jess recruited a colleague of hers that specialized in the type of surgery Patch needed. He agreed to take Patch as a patient, and the surgery went very well. Within a few days, Patch came home. She spent the next four weeks confined to a kennel so her back could heal. Every member of the sanctuary knew that Patch was unhappy. She barked, she bawled, and she bayed. That month stretched out forever, since nothing we tried consoled her. Finally, she made a full recovery, and I think even the old women celebrated her return to the pack.

Patch is still a resident at the sanctuary, and we celebrated her fourteenth birthday recently. Her eyesight and hearing have both faded with time. She suffers from a bit of arthritis in her back, but on most days,

she can be found flouncing around in the yard. She continues to poke her nose into everyone's business. Occasionally, a new member of the pack will take exception to her interference, but Patch has long since perfected her innocent escape. She still hassles the old women on the porch even though most of them, at this point, are younger than her. Patch's personality has not changed with the passing years. She truly never wanted to grow up, and we are so glad she didn't.

Taffy

Another double dapple puppy came into our lives later that same year. Both of Taffy's eyes were tiny and pink, and while she could recognize bright lights, she could see little else. Her cream colored coat had splashes of soft brown, and all four feet wore white socks.

Taffy was a baby and not just in age. The weather turned very cold the week she came to the sanctuary. The first morning I placed Taffy on my lap while I checked my email. She rooted around until she managed to crawl inside my robe. *Perfect spot to take a nap.* Every day for the next week, we repeated this practice. If I forgot, Taffy reminded me by standing on my feet and whining until I picked her up.

Taffy did not draw much attention on the website. I'm sure her disproportioned eyes had a lot to do with that. We did, nevertheless, receive two applications for her. The first one fell through when they asked us not to have her spayed, and the second one declined a home visit. After six months, it became apparent to Rick and me that Taffy would not be adopted. Her entire life had been spent here at the sanctuary, and we were not willing to risk her feeling abandoned by us. She became a permanent resident.

We knew that some dogs enjoyed socializing more than others. Cricket lived her life with us as a loner, and Mini rarely socializes with the other

dogs. But at such a young age, Taffy needed to be encouraged to take advantage of the benefits of joining the pack.

Once again, we faced a predicament that could only be solved by our dogs. We hoped that Gracie might once again work her magic, but she stayed fairly busy with Patch and Xera. The old girl's club on the back porch allowed Taffy to lay with them, but she rarely sought out their company on her own. Taffy certainly never showed any interest in the Rat Pack; wrestling held no allure for her. We averaged thirty-seven dogs at the sanctuary that spring, and we had no success at matching Taffy with any of them.

Around mid-summer, Baby Jade joined us. Baby Jade's birthday fell only a few days earlier than Taffy's. Baby Jade suffered with frequent seizures during the first six months of her life; therefore, we had to keep her in a sheltered area in our living room if we were unable to watch her. One afternoon, when Taffy's whimpering became more than I thought I could endure, I placed her with Baby Jade. They checked each other out thoroughly, then curled up together and promptly took a nap. *Success!*

Over the next weeks and months, Taffy became increasingly attached to her new friend. Baby Jade's seizures came under control, and autumn brought a reduction in the flow of new dogs in and out of the sanctuary. This allowed Taffy and Baby Jade to join the pack and enjoy the full freedom of the sanctuary. Baby Jade's life became full of birds to chase, the wading pool to enjoy, and regularly scheduled afternoon games of tug of war with Patch. Taffy's life became full of following Baby Jade everywhere she went. They both seemed satisfied with their arrangement. If Taffy became upset at another dog, she drew in closer to Baby Jade. The bond between these two puppies grew strong, and we rarely saw one without the other.

Baby Jade alerted us late one evening that something on the porch was not as it should be. Rick went out to check and found Taffy lifeless on their blanket. Baby Jade stood a few inches away barking and prodding at Taffy to get her up. She could not understand Taffy's failure to follow her to the doggie door like she had done for over eight years.

Taffy enjoyed near perfect health, and we never knew what took her from us. She remained a baby all those years, and ironically, she had found a new Momma in the form of Baby Jade.

Chapter 9

The Princess and the Puddinhead

After rescuing several hundred dogs over the past fifteen years, we needed my journals and our pictures to remember some of them. So many healthy, adoptable dogs came through our doors on their way to their forever homes that their faces and stories have faded a bit in our memories. The seniors who lived out their lives with us, some for only a short while, hold very special places in our hearts. But it's the special-needs

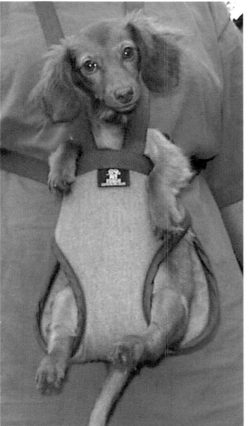

dogs that had to fight for a better quality to their lives that made the most profound impact on us. Mia and Milo are two dogs that we will never forget.

Mia came to us as a four-month-old, beautiful, red and blonde, longhair mini. She suffered from a condition that was new to us at the time called mega-esophagus. Her esophagus had a large pouch in it, caused by weak muscles, that could not push the food down into the stomach, much like a balloon, that has been inflated many times and then hangs limp. This condition causes dogs to regurgitate their food and water. Unfortunately, this food and water can often be aspirated into the lungs, causing pneumonia.

Mia's previous owners did not have the inclination to deal with this particular malady; they relinquished her to the sanctuary. After Doc Jess explained Mia's situation to me, I did a little research. I learned she had a much better chance at a healthy life if she ate in an upright position, allowing gravity to help move the food into her belly. So I began feeding her, while holding her in a vertical pose, up against my body. Ideally, she needed to remain erect for twenty to thirty minutes after each meal. This proved to be a difficult situation, as I rarely had the time to stand still for that amount of time. I searched for and found a shoulder harness that would hold Mia in the desired position. Even when I had to bend over, the harness swung away from my body keeping her straight up and down. *I do so love it when a plan comes together.* At four months old, Mia only weighed three and a half pounds, so carrying her was not a problem.

Each night, I soaked kibble in water to bring it to an oatmeal consistency for Mia to consume the next morning. I repeated this procedure after the morning meal so it was ready for Mia to eat in the evening. Her diet contained so much water that it minimized the amount she needed to drink during the day. This process, while not perfect, proved to be the best option for Mia, while still allowing me to care for the rest of the pack.

Mia was gorgeous. Her red hair sported blonde highlights around her ears and across her chest, framing her tiny face. When light shone into her eyes, they took on a pink hue that made her appear angelic. And that suited her well. Mia was delicate, and graceful. At times, her demeanor projected a shy, demure personality. At other times, she appeared flirtatious and coy. Her soft coat and tiny body made her a perfect cuddle partner, and we spoiled her rotten. She slept on Rick's pillow at night, with her body wrapped around his head. Occasionally, he would wake up with her feathered tail across his face, tickling his nose. She had become our little Princess.

Eight months after Mia became part of our lives, we received a call about another puppy that had been diagnosed with mega-esophagus. Milo also had an enlarged heart, and several veterinarians advised his owners to put him down; he had no chance at a quality life. As fate would have it, Milo was in College Station where our daughter, Jessica, attended TAMU. I was visiting her when we received the call. Jessica, our friend Melle Belle, and I made immediate plans to go and get this puppy. Within a few short hours, Milo was in my arms. Nothing about him gave any

indication that he was unhealthy. He had a short, black coat that glistened and long, beautiful dachshund ears. Milo, active and mischievous, played with a fervor that made me question his prognosis.

Doc Jess confirmed his diagnosis. She did not, however, concur with his death sentence. Milo began a regimen of heart meds, and we fed him just like we had learned to do with Mia. At only three pounds, Milo lived in perpetual motion. He gave Patch a run for her money, as the pack busybody. I worried that he would get himself into trouble because he stuck his nose into everybody's business. But the pack accepted Milo and brushed off his intrusions with little difficulty. Rick began to call him Milo, Pilo, the Puddinhead.

Our radiant Princess and our rambunctious Puddinhead became fast friends. I don't know if their friendship flourished because of their physical size or their physical ailments. They both knew that they could only eat one at a time in my harness. They both knew that they had full privileges on our laps. And they both knew that Rick's pillow was only big enough for the two of them, with a tiny bit left over for Rick to enjoy.

Mia and Milo enjoyed celebrity status everywhere they went. In the vet clinic waiting room, they shared center stage. At fund raising events in the local pet stores they drew crowds of admirers. And the page they shared on our website racked up more hits than any other. So naturally, I purchased several matching outfits for their public appearances.

After a few years, Milo began to have some bad days. His labored breathing and listless attitude worried us. With adjustments to his heart medication, thankfully, those days were few and far between for many years. Mia contracted pneumonia a few times, but we caught it early, and she recovered quickly on the proper antibiotics. During times of illness for either dog, the other stayed close by their side.

For eight years, we relished their lives and their love for each other. Then, tragically, Mia became extremely ill. Her kidneys were failing. Her chances of recovery were small, and Rick and I began to grieve. She only lasted a few more days. Our precious Princess Mia died with Rick's arms around her and my arms around him.

Milo's health deteriorated over the following weeks. Rick and I knew he grieved his sweet Princess and all we could do was hold him. But like the little trooper he had always been, Milo slowly recovered physically. Emotionally, he never bounced back completely. His interest in the other dogs' lives waned tremendously. For another two years he continued to bark and run

through the yard on warm days. On cold days, he chose to stay inside on the pillow he shared with Rick.

In his eleventh year, Milo took a sudden turn for the worse. His symptoms included lethargy, vomiting, and blood in his stools. Doc Jess diagnosed him with Addison's disease. Although rare in dogs, Addison's can be more likely in dogs with mega-esophagus. Milo's adrenal glands no longer produced enough of a certain hormone that his body needed. His hair became chalky and eventually began to fall out. He no longer ran in the yard and only went outside briefly to do his business and occasionally lay in the sunshine.

Milo survived another nine months on the medication he received to help replace those hormones. Then one day in late November of 2015, he went outside and lay down in the sun for the last time. Rick buried Milo beside Mia. Our Princess and our Puddinhead will forever be together, in our hearts and in our minds.

Chapter 10
The Home of the Brave

Courage comes in many forms. Most of our long term residents have faced adversity, and they responded with a strength of character that is inspiring. All of our special-needs dogs get up each morning and face a challenging day. Three dogs that showed impressive valor during their time with us deserve to be singled out.

Nate

Nate came out of the shelter in San Angelo in August of 2001. He suffered from canine dwarfism. His legs were abnormally short and bowed, and only measured two and a half inches. His coat had multiple bald areas where the skin had become dark and wrinkled. His wide feet turned out in the front, and he sounded like he was snoring all the time. His initial blood work showed that he also had thyroid problems. He began thyroid medications, and it took several months to get those treatments regulated.

During those first few months, Nate also suffered seizures. I kept him close. *I didn't have to try very hard, because his favorite chair was the top of my shoes.*

Nate picked out a favorite spot beside me on the bed where I watched television in the evenings. When Rick came home and approached me, Nate became very protective. I had to hold on to him long enough to get a kiss from my husband without Nate taking a bite out of Rick's face. Nate loved Rick, but only if I wasn't around. Rick nicknamed him Nater the Alligator because his jaws stayed ready to snap.

It didn't surprise me when Nate began to show signs of a Napoleon complex. He constantly stayed on the lookout for any slight to his manhood. This condition, according to Rick, only reared its ugly head when I was close by. Nate did not want any other dogs on my lap or even close to my feet. That might have caused some serious situations with some of our young males, but thankfully Nate grunted and snarled, more than he bit. The other dogs soon learned that Nate didn't present much of a threat, and they mostly ignored his show of aggression.

Nate loved sweaters. Most of our dogs could not get them off quickly enough. Because Nate remained bald most of his life, those sweaters served as his coat. He spent a large part of his life in a sweater, and I kept plenty of them around. One winter we experienced some difficulty with our heater, and I spent three days feeding wood into the fireplace while trying to keep sweaters on the seniors. They could not understand the need, and I found empty sweaters all over the sanctuary. Nate, on the other hand, never took his sweater off, and his favorite was always the one fresh out of the dryer.

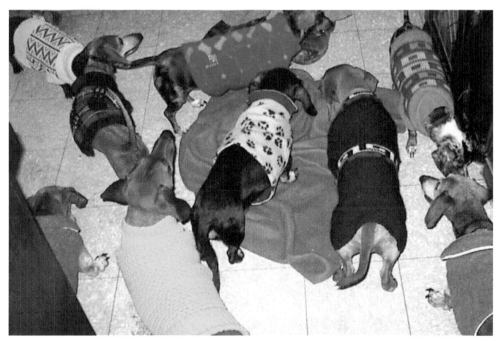

Some dogs display a unique gait in their movements. Patch held the number one spot in that category until Nate arrived. He would take two steps forward and then one back. Or he slid sideways, and his back feet stepped around in a circle until he faced the other direction. Nate had a certain rhythm to his steps, and I wondered what music must be playing in his mind. I have very few memories of Nate running forward. His destination could rarely be determined, because he often changed his trajectory in mid-stride. I'm not a dancer, but I believe Nate might have been practicing the Cha Cha. *Cuban bloodline maybe?*

While Nate's courage on the surface appeared to be mostly false bravado, he conquered multiple disabilities every day. I grew accustomed to having that little sweater covered tube cuddled next to me in bed each night. When we lost Nate, only three years after he came to the sanctuary, I missed his pig like snorts, his unpredictable strides, and his ten foot tall attitude. Rick buried Nate in his favorite sweater, fresh from the dryer.

Gus

Gus came to us in June of 2002 from a veterinarian in Houston. After having damaged his back, Gus went through an unsuccessful surgery to correct the problem, and ended up with a wheeled cart that restored his mobility. His original owners opted to have Gus put down, but Dr. Andrea convinced them to sign away their rights of ownership. Dr. Andrea allowed Gus to live at her clinic for several months before she sought out a more permanent home for that spirited guy. When Rick and I agreed to take Gus, we had no experience with wheeled dog carts. Dr. Andrea adored Gus enough to make the ten hour drive to deliver him to the sanctuary personally. Gus came to us with his made-to-order cart,

and Dr. Andrea showed us how it worked.

With an almost solid black coat and two brown eyebrows, I would have named him Bandit. But we always used our dogs given names if we knew them. Dr. Andrea put Gus in his cart, and she had just finished strapping him in when he took off through the house. I tried to concentrate on the information that Dr. Andrea prepared for us while Rick followed our new speed demon through the house. Gus maneuvered that cart like a pro. He backed up, turned corners, and stopped on a dime. Exploring our house had Gus completely occupied. It was all we could do to get him to be still for a goodbye kiss from the lady that had truly saved his life.

Our long term pack members had become accustomed to having new dogs introduced to their world. After Dr. Andrea left, Rick opened the doggie door, and the dogs started pouring in one after another. The Rat Pack performed their ritualistic sniffing of the new guy from stem to stern, paying special attention to his wheels. Next, the old ladies took their turn and their time inspecting Gus. Finally, the old men walked past him, with only a hint of interest. I remember thinking how proud Gus stood with his head held high. Everyone had their turn familiarizing themselves with Gus; everyone but Patch.

As usual, Patch came onto the scene last with mischief on her mind. She waggled up in front of Gus, sniffed his face a few times, briefly checked out his cart, and then nose butted him right in the chest. Gus took a few steps back. Patch took off running sideways through the den, into the kitchen, and out the doggie door. Gus was right behind her the entire way until his wheels hit the side of the doggie door and stopped him in

his tracks. We had a Three Stooges type pile up when the Rat Pack and all the other dogs slammed into Gus' cart and each other. Rick and I laughed about that collision for hours.

Rick pulled Gus out of the doggie door, escorted him back into the den, and out onto the porch. I was just about to warn Rick about the drop going off the porch, when Gus flew off the concrete and hit the grass running. For two hours, Gus ran up and down the full hundred foot length of our yard. At one point he ran so fast that he miscalculated his turn a bit, and his right wheel bounced off the tile fence as he came out of his turn. The Rat Pack loved it and ran right along side this new, cool kid with his own cart. The cart was well-built, and that proved to be very important; Gus had a need for speed.

After evening chores, I found Gus in the middle of the grass with most of the other dogs around him. Everyone's tongues hung out of their mouths, and I knew we would all get some sleep that night. I unstrapped Gus from his cart and took him inside to rinse him off. He slept with a diaper on, inside a large laundry basket, laying on the blanket Dr. Andrea had delivered with him.

I spent the next few days working out the routine of care for Gus, and he spent those days running. The Rat Pack finally quit bolting through the yard behind Gus and went back to their normal lives. Gus spent several hours in his cart every morning and then came inside to be out of the cart for most of the afternoon. He was always ready to get back into that cart by late afternoon, and often I would have to chase him down to finish strapping him in. Gus had what Dr. Andrea had wanted for him all along: room to enjoy the freedom his cart provided.

Gus' high speed life caused more than one collision when he plowed through a wrestling match or a dog took an unfortunate turn into his path. But everyone adapted to the new normal, and even Xera soon acquired the skills to stay out of Gus' way. He and Patch enjoyed multiple games of chase each day. I would have put my money on Gus if I just considered speed, but Patch had two cards up her sleeve. Because of the way Patch ran, Gus could never tell which direction she was actually heading, and Patch had the doggie door as an escape hatch. It became a common occurrence for us to hear Gus crash his wheels into that doggie door, and eventually he learned to back out of it himself. Our backyard runs east and west, with one leg off to the north beside the kitchen. Gus rolled his cart a few times before he began to regulate his speed through the turn. Rick informed me that Gus had also learned to lean into the corners.

Over the coming months, we adjusted Gus' routine several times. His enthusiasm for full motion in his cart began to cause some lesions on his back legs where they rested on the pads. We tried wrapping Gus' back feet and legs with gauze or ace bandages, but the other dogs wouldn't leave the wraps alone. He was forced at that point to stay out of his cart for awhile, but he still needed to be active. So I came up with a plan that allowed him to go outside, without his cart. I bought several new-born

baby nightgowns that protected Gus' back legs. His front legs fit through the sleeves in the nightgown, a diaper kept him clean, and Gus could still fly.

The summer of 2002 brought a swarm of new dogs to the sanctuary, and I welcomed additional alternatives to simplify Gus' care. Rick covered the pads on his cart with sheepskin which allowed him to go back to using his cart, part time. Rick also adapted a leather skid for Gus from an old welder's apron that attached around his shoulders. His back legs rested on the leather when he ran, and that protected his tender skin. A combination of all three of the systems at Gus' disposal became our answer, and Gus split his time between the cart, the nightgowns, and the leather skid. And much to Patch's surprise, Gus enjoyed full access to the doggie door when he was not in his cart. Catching Patch no longer posed a problem for Gus.

Gus was four years old when he came into our lives. He lived another five years, running and enjoying the yard, weather allowing. When rain or snow kept Gus inside all day, he pouted. Just like most of our Dachshunds, Gus loved to be snuggled up under blankets. One rainy day in December of 2008, Gus crawled under a blanket in our den, and I found him there, lifeless, a few hours later. Rick and I grieved his loss, but we drew great comfort from our memories of Gus flying through the yard. *I'm gonna do what they say can't be done, I'm eastbound, just watch ol' Bandit run!*

Duke

In the Spring of 2015, Doc Jess called to discuss a male Dachshund that had been diagnosed with an aggressive form of bone cancer. The pregnant owner did not feel she could deal with Duke's illness and proposed that he be put down. Doc Jess offered to take over his care, and custody of Duke was signed over to her. When asked if we could take on this sweet little man, Rick and I did not hesitate to agree.

I met Duke the next morning and was surprised to see a healthy, active dog. He had a small tumor on the left side of his chest. Doc Jess explained his cancer to me and made it clear he was facing a tough fight. We agreed that Rick and I were going to care for Duke, and Doc Jess would be responsible for his medical expenses.

Duke underwent surgery to remove the tumor, and by four the next afternoon he came home to the sanctuary. I prepared a pen for him in the den to use as a recovery space. As a two-year-old Duke recovered from the surgery quickly. Within a few days he felt well enough to play in the yard. Friendly and lovable, Duke fit in with the pack immediately. Rick and I loved every minute of his fun and hoped we were looking at his future.

Every evening I brought Duke to our room to spend more time with us. He sat up proud and strong, and rarely showed any signs of pain. Duke and Delilah became good friends, and they shared her pillow on the bed. Duke barked and howled along with all the other dogs, and ran from one side of the bed to the other to keep a close eye on Jake and Gena. When Delilah took off running down the hall, Duke stood at the edge of the bed and barked until she returned to sit beside him.

Duke endured three surgeries over the next two months, and each time his recovery was harder. Tragically, Duke's tumors returned within a few weeks after each surgery. Doc Jess tried several different chemotherapy drugs including a new one that was injected directly into the tumors. But nothing could stop the onslaught of his disease.

It became apparent when Duke's pain remained hard to manage ten days after his last surgery, that he could not go on. I made the decision to end his courageous battle, and I held him for the last time that next day.

Duke's struggles were not in vain. Doc Jess gained valuable experience that will no doubt benefit other dogs. Rick and I learned the joy and heartache of hospice care in its most concentrated form. Caring for a dying dog was not new for us. Duke's story, however, started out with little hope and never gained any positive traction. We measured his short life in moments, and we cherished each and every one.

Chapter 11

Don't Even Think About Touching Me

Most of the dogs that came to us labeled as un-adoptable either suffered from a serious physical illness or were simply old and considered undesirable. Once in awhile, our efforts were challenged with a dog that had emotional issues. These dogs demanded our constant attention. We could not always count on our pack therapy theory, or at least not initially. We had to learn as we went along how to deal with overwhelming fear, aggression, and/or neurotic behavior. While failure was never an option in our minds, these dogs tested our limits of patience and knowledge. We were determined not to allow any long term isolation solutions. We believed that the happiness of our dogs depended more on their support for one another than any efforts Rick and I could produce.

Macy Laura

Macy came to us from a shelter that was two hundred miles from the sanctuary. She had been found tied to the shelter door, and she bit two employees before they could get her into a kennel. When the director called me, she had just about convinced herself that euthanasia was the only option for this aggressive female. I assured her we would be willing to work with Macy, and that our sanctuary provided a unique opportunity for her to have a life. She agreed to give Macy that chance.

David and I arrived at the shelter before noon the next day. Seeing the muzzle on Macy's face saddened me, but I believed it would soon be unnecessary. She had short red hair sprinkled with a tint of blonde. Her long ears and slender nose produced an aristocratic look that we later discovered matched her personality. Macy had current rabies tags and a scar to prove she had been spayed. Someone had, at one time, loved this dog.

One of our bedrooms had been equipped with everything a dog might need to settle in. I had Macy out of the crate and in this isolation room by the time Rick arrived home from work. We tried numerous times that evening to get Macy to allow us to hold her. A low growl rumbled from her chest as Rick tried to soothe her with his soft words.

As long as we stayed on the other side of the room, Macy ignored us. Our instincts told us that if we could hold her, we could comfort her. We both tried several times to approach her. She ran. Then we moved towards her with our eyes averted. She ran. Next, Rick tried a tactic that he had used successfully with other frightened animals. He sat down on the floor with his back to her. After he remained completely still for several moments, he edged his way in her direction. Macy let him get within a few feet of her, then he turned, and she ran. Repeated attempts of that same maneuver always produced the same results.

Several days passed with no success at getting closer to Macy. Finally, one day Rick walked methodically in her direction with his hands behind his back. Motionless, but vigilant, Macy watched Rick. She allowed him to get right beside her, and he knelt down just a few feet from her. She did not run. Macy stood very still until Rick slid his hands from behind his back, then she bolted across the floor. And we knew. Macy hated hands. *But if we couldn't touch her, how could we possibly love on her enough?*

Our isolation room has a low window that looks out onto the back porch, where the other dogs play and lounge in the afternoons. We soon discovered that Macy spent a lot of time looking out that window, wagging her tail like crazy. *I would have bet the farm her blood pressure and heart rate went down as she watched the other dogs.* Now we had two important pieces to the Macy puzzle: she hated hands, and she longed to be with the pack.

So we introduced Macy to Nurse Gracie. The two of them seemed perfectly at ease together, and we moved forward with our plans to introduce her to the other residents of the sanctuary. After the first few weeks with the pack, it became apparent to Rick and me that while Macy enjoyed the other dogs around her, she held little interest in interacting with any of the them. She held herself aloft, seemingly looking down that long nose in judgement of the other dogs. This trait became quite comical to watch as Macy scrutinized the goings on around her. She often investigated the play and interaction among the other dogs, made a judgement that such things were beneath her status, and walked away with her head pointing to the sky.

Getting Macy to the vet the first time presented a bit of a problem. The only solution I could come up with had already proven useful in our everyday life. Many of our dogs had their own kennel that they slept in at night. Macy slept in one on our bedroom dresser and seemed to really enjoy that high perch. Originally, I coaxed her into the kennel by placing it on the floor with a treat visible in the back. She pranced right in. I closed the kennel and picked it up to rest on the dresser. Within a few days, the treat became unnecessary as Macy voluntarily walked in every time I gave her access. We called that kennel her throne room, as she used it to survey her subjects on the ground.

Now I had an easy way to transport her, but I still needed to ensure she would allow herself to be examined once I delivered her to the clinic. After discussing the situation with Doc Jess, she suggested we use a little pill called Ace. I called it our nighty-night pill, and I could give it to Macy in a spoonful of peanut butter an hour or so before our appointment. Thankfully, this solution worked like a charm. Macy became groggy enough that she could be handled.

Over the next few months, Macy revealed distinct characteristics of obsessive compulsive behavior. She often appeared to be hunting; she stood in one corner for an extended amount of time, whimpering. Our other dogs ultimately learned to dismiss these actions, but Rick and I grew anxious. When her obsessive ways escalated to gnawing on her hip enough to open a wound, we again sought out medical advice. By this time, Doc Jess and I had established a trusting relationship that allowed her to diagnose and treat Macy almost entirely on my description of her behavior. At the clinic, the nighty-night pill diluted the worst of her psychosis; the open wounds spoke for themselves.

Doc Jess began a treatment of clomipramine to calm Macy down. While it helped quell her degree of fixation, her chewing didn't completely stop. Several times over the years we found it necessary to take drastic steps to prevent her from injuring herself. An E-collar eliminated her access to her hip but it caused her whining to increase. Elevating the dose of her meds helped, but it took the joy out of her life. Nothing solved the problem permanently.

Rick and I loved Macy for seven years. Her beautiful coat of red and blonde eventually became salted with gray. We managed her emotional waves to the best of our abilities, and Macy rewarded us with a decreasing fear of our touch. She ultimately allowed us to pick her up to place her in her kennel to eat or sleep. And while she had a way of dancing around to get our attention, she never really craved our touch. Macy remained unique in our rescue experiences, and we still laugh when we remember her elitist attitude. At the estimated age of ten, heart disease stole her quality of life. Macy passed away in her throne room one night. Rick and I knew we had done our best for her. We had not cured all her ills, but we provided the loving, constant care that allowed her to live out her life in comfort.

Brownie

Snow and ice covered our world the day I got a call from a frantic lady just miles from our sanctuary. She had acquired a Dachshund from a local breeder. The breeder told her the little guy didn't meet her standards, so she volunteered to give him away at no charge. After only a few days, this distraught lady knew Brownie would never be able to stay with her family. Brownie had struck out at everyone. I tried to put her off for a few days so the roads could clear up, but she begged me to come right away. So I went after him, knowing his actions could best be described as extremely intolerable, and perhaps unrepairable. I wondered, but never found out, how that lady had gotten Brownie home without getting bitten. *Perhaps I wasn't the only one with access to nighty-night pills.*

Brownie's owner donned a pair of leather welding gloves to carry him out to my car that afternoon. He growled and snapped as she placed him in the kennel. As usual, our refuge already overflowed with dogs. We had a dog in our isolation room and a new mom and her puppies in our spare room. Our back bathroom was unoccupied, and that would have to be Brownie's place until we could evaluate his needs. I carried his kennel to the bathroom and worried if I could get him out without getting attacked. Luckily for me, he desperately wanted out of that cage. Brownie immediately ran behind the toilet the minute I opened the door. I placed food and water bowls right inside the door for him. Overwhelmed with the sheer numbers of residents in our sanctuary, I had to leave him for Rick to deal with.

Unfortunately, Rick's work kept him away from home until late that night. His exhaustion prevented him from visiting with Brownie. The next day, I decided to see if I might make a little headway with this dog. The minute I walked into that bathroom, Brownie ran for the safety behind the toilet. I refilled his food and water and sat down across the room. For a brief moment he appeared to be ignoring me, desiring instead to make himself as invisible as possible. I talked to him, hoping to begin what was obviously going to be a long period of therapy. He answered me with a snarl and a show of beautiful, white teeth. It didn't take me long to realize his problems were out of my league. Brownie would have to wait to see what Rick could do.

The next afternoon, Rick came home anxious to meet Brownie. We went together into the bathroom and positioned ourselves across the room from our little frightened rescue. He alternated between a low growl and a pitiful whine. Rick never made a move that day to get closer to Brownie. He recognized that the task before him to rehabilitate this dog could be colossal. And he was right. Five days passed before Rick could even inch a little bit closer to Brownie, without him becoming frantic.

After ten days, Rick decided to step up his game. He started out just a few feet from the corner where Brownie sat, shaking and grumbling. Slowly, Rick moved closer. When he was directly in front of the toilet, Rick tossed a liver treat to Brownie. It laid on the floor inches from Brownie, and his little nose twitched as he tried to muster the courage to take it. Rick threw another treat right beside the first one, and that scared little dog gave in to temptation. He snatched them both up and retreated to the farthest possible spot away from Rick. Finally, we felt a bit of progress had been made.

Over the next week, I became completely crushed with chores. The litter of puppies had to be weaned, the little one in the isolation room joined the pack, and two more young dogs moved into the isolation room. The only contact I had with Brownie was during feeding time. He showed no signs of warming up to me. Rick visited with him for at least an hour each evening, and at last began to report some gradual improvement.

Twenty days from the day that we first met Brownie, Rick called down the hall for me to come into the bathroom. I opened the door to see that beautiful red dog standing on Rick's shoulders. With two feet on each shoulder, Brownie stood calm and collected when I entered the room. I squealed with delight which caused Brownie to bolt back to his hiding place in the corner. Rick gave me a disappointed look that sent me scrambling from the room.

After learning my lesson about screeching, Rick and I returned together to see Brownie the next evening. I stayed by the door while Rick took his spot across the room. I could hear Brownie's tail hitting the wall, as he wagged it with delight. Rick tossed him a treat; he ate it quickly. Then, as if he had been doing so all along, he walked onto Rick's lap and leaped onto his shoulders. He stood for awhile, then proceeded to lie down with his body circling Rick's head. He finally felt at ease. I had almost given up hope that Brownie's rehab would ever advance this far. I should have

known not to doubt Rick's abilities to reach even the most disturbed animal. But for Rick, Brownie's tremendous improvement seemed like an unreachable goal. While Rick and I reveled in the success of the moment, we couldn't help but wonder if Brownie had any idea how life changing his new found trust in Rick could be.

The next, and perhaps more daunting task concerning Brownie, would be to find him a home. We did not feel it wise to try to integrate this little guy into our pack, and we could not keep him in that bathroom forever. So I contacted our many rescue friends, searching for what must be the perfect home. Kate put Brownie's bio up on our website. The appropriate home for him would be with a man; a single man with no pets and no children. Within a few days, the ideal application came into my email. A gentleman in south Texas, who had been in a wheelchair for most of his life, wanted a chance to meet Brownie. I quickly arranged for a rescuer close by to do the home visit. The report I received within a few days seemed almost too good to be true. This man lived in a duplex with a small fenced in yard. His parents lived next door, and his older brother was a veterinarian. As fate would have it, this application was the only one we received for Brownie. Immediately, Rick made arrangements to take Brownie to meet his potential new owner. I would have loved to be there for that placement, but my situation with a flood of dogs kept me at the sanctuary.

The following Saturday, Rick and Brownie left early for the four hour drive. Rick met the entire family in the front yard of the duplex that afternoon. They all agreed that Rick should introduce Brownie to his new owner, Jack, one on one. Rick and Jack visited for a while with Brownie draped across Rick's shoulders.

Within an hour, Rick excused himself for a minute and left Brownie in the chair next to Jack's wheelchair. When Rick returned to the room, Brownie's eyes remained on Jack. Rick took his cue to stand back and watch. Jack spoke to Brownie as if they had been friends forever. His patience astonished Rick, and undoubtedly encouraged Brownie. Within a few minutes, Brownie stood on the arm of the wheelchair allowing Jack to scratch his ears. And then, as if it were always meant to be, he leapt into Jack's lap. By the time Rick left Jack's home that evening, Brownie was standing on Jack's shoulders. The connection Rick made with that supposedly unrepairable dog, had re-wired Brownie.

We received updates from Jack and Brownie for years following that placement. They lived and loved each other as true and strong as any man and his dog possibly could. Jack assured us that Brownie had added great pleasure and meaning to his life. Rick and I knew that Brownie's true purpose had been met the day he learned to love Jack.

Cricket

Cricket came into our lives at the age of ten from a Humane Society in south Texas. She had a tiny frame that carried entirely too much weight, and she suffered from multiple benign fatty tumors. Doc Jess removed the tumors right away, and Cricket began to lose some weight. As was so often the case, we had no background information on her.

During her mandatory isolation period, we learned that Cricket did not want to be touched. We hoped that once her incisions from her surgery healed she might become a little easier to handle, but that did not happen. Rick tried for weeks, without any success, to get Cricket to allow him to hold her. Cricket never showed any indication of aggression, so we hoped the pack might heal her fears. Sadly, that did not happen either. She remained a loner. Eventually, she allowed me to handle her briefly to put her in a kennel to eat. Cricket loved meal time and garnered some enjoyment from walking the backyard and stretching out in the sun.

Never once did we see her play with another dog. Never once did we see her wag her tail. Never once were we allowed to show her any affection. For the entire two years that Cricket lived here with us, we felt the sting of failure when we looked at her. We desperately wanted to improve on the quality of her life. Inevitably, we had to accept the fact that we had done the best we could for her. Some problems had no solutions. Cricket lived her life on her own terms, and she laid down in the yard one day and crossed the Rainbow Bridge alone.

Chapter 12
Maximum Capacity

We opened our sanctuary in July of 2001. Midsummer is rush season for rescue groups. People change jobs, move out of town, and take extended vacations during the summer. That mobility provides opportunities for their pets to become unwanted anchors. The summer months also signaled the time when puppies, given as Christmas presents, turned into unruly teenagers. Unfortunately, many end up in shelters (or worse) during the following summer.

Our number of residents could rise and fall as rapidly as the tides. Many of the adoptable dogs that we rescued found their permanent homes quickly. Others were transferred to rescuers that needed to place a senior or a special-needs dog with us. During 2002, fifty-five new dogs came through the sanctuary. Thirty-one of those dogs found new homes. Twenty-four seniors and special-needs dogs found their forever home with us during those twelve months, and we grieved the loss of nine sweet souls.

2003 brought another barrage of new dogs our way. The sanctuary rescued forty-six dogs that year, and we hit our all time high of fifty-seven dogs by mid-July. We found new homes for or transferred thirty-two dogs by Christmas. Thirteen seniors or special-needs dogs came into our lives and, sadly, Rick added twelve little graves to our cemetery that year.

Late in June of 2003, I participated in the dismantling of a puppy mill located a hundred miles from us. On that day, I brought home fourteen five-year-old Dachshunds, who had never touched grass, had rarely been held, had never been named, and had never been loved. Puppy mill dogs often had tattooed numbers in their ears for identification. I remember taking them in groups of three and four dogs to the vet each day for a week. I took a list of names that corresponded with the number of males and females and asked the vet techs to assign names to the dogs as they received their vet care. Before that huge rescue, I personally named all the dogs that came to us from shelters, puppy mills, or off the streets. These dogs received new names to begin their new lives. Receiving fourteen dogs all at once, however, overpowered me, and I had no time to worry with matching names to dogs personalities.

That first, and most horrific, contact with a true puppy mill tainted our perception of human nature. Twenty-nine adult dogs and five litters of puppies came out of that place that day, and everyone involved had tear stained faces before we managed to leave. The females were well fed, especially the ones with litters. The males didn't fare as well. The cages were filthy, and the smell knocked us down when we first went inside. All of the females had mammary tumors. Most of the males showed some degree of aggression, certainly where their food was concerned. Three of the fourteen dogs succumbed to cancer before they could reach their permanent homes. The hopelessness of those pitiful, but precious lives, inside that "little family business" leaked into our souls like nothing else we had ever experienced.

The atmosphere here at the sanctuary changed to a frantic pace, and Rick and I both went to bed each night exhausted. We had dogs in every area of the sanctuary. All of the puppy mill males had to be separated from each other and from our current residents. The females, exhausted from their years of one litter after another, slept a good part of their days. When they weren't asleep, they reveled in the grass and the attention. I had to write their new names on their collars just to try to keep them straight. Rick spent every evening working with the males, one at a time. They grew to love him, and he worked miracles with them. All four of the males went to a home where they would be the only pet, so they could receive the personal attention they desperately needed.

I spent two hours each morning just getting everyone fed. They each had to be placed in a kennel with their food, and we didn't own fifty-seven kennels. It took two shifts to get everyone fed. I also spent at least an hour each morning and each evening with Mia or Milo hanging from my shoulders after their meals. All fourteen of the puppy mill dogs received medications for the first week. Add that to the eight dogs already in residence that received daily medications, and that consumed another hour of my morning. Countless hours each day had to be devoted to cleaning kennels, raking the yard, washing food and water bowls, washing blankets, transporting dogs back and forth from the vet, and trying to love on all the dogs. And I needed to get good pictures of each of the new dogs, as well as write up their bios.

Kate worked overtime to update the website, and Charlotte spent countless hours contacting rescuers to help me disperse these new dogs. That ended up being one of the hardest tasks involved with this influx of puppy mill dogs; all the rescuers in our sphere were already overloaded due to the summer deluge. Thankfully, many of our closest rescue buddies understood the need to step up their efforts. Everyone benefited from the success of our sanctuary, and we all pulled together to work through each hurdle we faced. The dedication of four or five people saved our sanity during that difficult time.

Three days before a huge transport to meet a California rescuer, I received a call from Mitzi. She had taken on my roll of walking the local shelters at least once a week to check for Dachshunds in need. She found two bonded Dachshunds that only had one more day to leave the shelter alive. Mitzi named these two little wire hair females Buffy and Jodie, and I needed to go after them the next morning. When I arrived at the shelter, the receptionist informed me that one of those dogs was pregnant and ready to give birth. I laughed, and cried, at the same time and excused myself for a few minutes to regain my composure. On the way home, I realized that there was only one unoccupied space left for these two ladies, our bathroom. By lunch time, I had them settled with a birthing box full of clean rags and the last two blankets in the house for beds. At midnight, Jodie went into labor. In all my years I had never witnessed the birth of any animal, and my raw emotions got the best of me. I cried like a baby for the hour it took Jodie to give birth to six

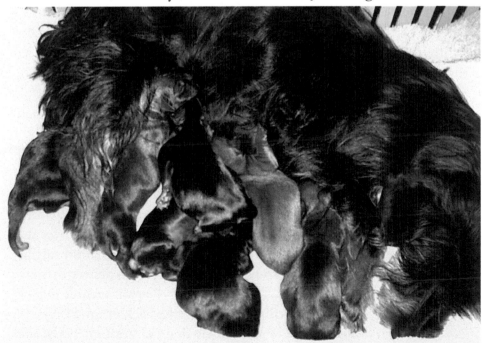

beautiful, healthy, puppies; our total population swelled to fifty-seven. Buffy, the companion dog, helped Jodie clean her puppies, and they both curled up in the birthing box as I closed the door and crawled to my bed at 2:00 a.m.

The next morning arrived way before I liked, but the dogs had already started barking, and I could hear the puppies squeaking through the bathroom door. I had hours of chores ahead of me on top of preparing for the transport, planned for the next day at 5:00 a.m. I had to get paperwork together for the dogs I was taking to Albuquerque. Eight of the puppy mill dogs were scheduled for this transport, along with three other adoptable dogs. Thankfully, all four of the puppy mill males would be on their way to happy lives. That freed up quite a bit of space and eliminated a huge amount of work maneuvering the dogs between kennels and isolation rooms.

Rick came home around 6:00 p.m. and hit the ground running to help me prepare. I wanted all eleven kennels loaded in my car before I went to bed. Rick washed and loaded them while I made last minute phone calls to get directions to our meeting place. I also had to type up instructions for Rick to handle the feeding and the meds while I made the run. I set my alarm for 4:00 a.m. I'm not sure my head hit the pillow before I fell asleep.

Rick helped me load the dogs the next morning, and by 5:30 a.m. my brother David and I headed west to Albuquerque. The drive would take six hours if we drove straight through, but we needed to stop twice to let the dogs out of the kennels. We picked rest areas with trees and plenty of room to set up two wire pens that I shuffled the dogs in and out of. David walked the males, individually, while I made sure everyone had access to fresh water.

We arrived in Albuquerque around 1:00 p.m. It took us another half hour to find the park where the meeting would take place. Kathleen, our California rescue friend, arrived about an hour later. The dogs had all enjoyed a nice walk in the park, and we didn't waste any time loading them into Kathleen's van. She and I spent a few minutes going over the paperwork. I attached a picture of each dog to their vaccination certificates and spay/neuter records, so Kathleen was all set to deliver them to her rescue group in San Diego. David and I left the park at three o'clock with eleven empty kennels rattling quietly in the back of my SUV.

The tension of the last few weeks slowly drained from my body, and soon David and I laughed and talked as the miles flew by. We stopped for a nice dinner that contrasted drastically with the packed sandwiches I brought with us for lunch. At 11:00 p.m. that night, I dropped David off at home, and drove the few blocks back to the sanctuary.

Rick had taken a very rare second day off, and he fed the dogs the next morning, allowing me to stay in bed late. I think the dogs were happy to see me when I finally got up. I know I enjoyed seeing only forty-six of them waiting for me to pass out daily hugs.

By the middle of August, when things slowed down in the rescue world, we placed six more dogs in forever homes. The puppies grew quickly, and before they had all been spayed/neutered we had homes waiting for them as well. Soon after that, Buffy and Jodie went to a wonderful home together, and by Halloween we only had thirty-two residents in the sanctuary. In contrast to my days in July, my chores seemed like a breeze.

Then our lives turned upside-down again. A rescuer from New Mexico delivered two senior dogs to our sanctuary just days before Thanksgiving. Unfortunately, we had somehow gotten our wires crossed in our communications of these dogs' backgrounds. We did not find out until three days later that they had come directly from the shelter to our sanctuary. She had assured me they had been in isolation for two weeks, but she did not tell me that isolation had taken place inside the shelter.

I woke up on Friday after Thanksgiving to the sound of multiple dogs coughing. Both of the new dogs came down with kennel cough, and they had been mingling with my pack for seventy-two hours! Several of my seniors also began to cough, and I made a frantic call to Doc Jess. She wanted to see the new dogs and any others I was especially concerned about. I decided to take Charlie because of his congestive heart condition, Milo because of his enlarged heart, and the new senior ladies. We waited in the car until Doc Jess could see us, so we wouldn't risk exposing any animals in her waiting room. Within a few minutes, we were taken in through the side door straight to the exam room.

Charlie already showed symptoms of kennel cough, and Doc Jess did blood work on him. His blood showed signs of a secondary infection caused by the kennel cough. Charlie and both of the new females were prescribed a round of antibiotics. I picked up some cough medicine and some honey to help soothe the throats of the infected dogs. Although isolation would probably not help us now, I moved all the dogs with symptoms into one isolation room. Kennel cough is extremely contagious, and everyone had already been exposed. Isolating the ill dogs helped make us feel like we were doing everything possible to protect our pack. I began to dose out the honey, diluted with a bit of water. The dogs with the worst of the coughs received cough medicine every four hours.

For ten days, I emptied and sterilized the water bowls all over the sanctuary three times per day. I mopped the floors every day with bleach, and I continuously washed all blankets and bedding materials. To help break up the congestion in their lungs, the dogs with the worst coughs all spent some time in the little bathroom with the hot water running until the room filled with steam.

Most of the dogs seemed to be doing better by the end of that first ten days. Three more dogs moved into the isolation room, before I finally began to believe we had stopped the spread. Milo, thank heavens, never showed any sign of infection. Ginger and Ariel (the two infected new dogs) progressed quickly with the antibiotics and rest. Charlie suffered the most, and some effects of his illness never subsided. The cough he already had from his congestive heart condition worsened during his isolation, and he never regained all the ground he lost during those weeks before Christmas.

At some point during the kennel cough ordeal, I contacted the rescuer that brought the ill dogs to us. She truly did not know the danger to which she had exposed our fragile dogs. She offered to cover our vet expenses, and I asked her to just make a donation to the sanctuary. Within a week, we received a check and a huge box of brand new stainless steel feeding bowls from her. I still use those bowls today.

We learned a few very hard lessons in 2003. First, we learned that sometimes we had to say no, even if our hearts disagreed. Second, the road to Albuquerque is quite long with eleven dogs in tow. Third, every new dog would go into isolation unless we knew for sure there could be no chance of exposure to kennel cough. And fourth, new life is always a miracle, no matter what the circumstances. *Oh, and by the way, Jessica and I named those six puppies, Hope, Valor, Faith, Joy, Charity, and Bob!*

Chapter 13
The Bash

Over the years, we received many boxes of donated supplies. Gaye sends several boxes of crocheted blankets every year. Another supporter sent a huge box of collars and leashes, a fellow rescuer sent forty stainless steel feeding bowls, Charlotte sent a wonderful pen made from PVC pipe that served as our recovery ward, and Dave sent a set of gorgeous Dachshund plates to adorn our walls. Early in the summer of 2004, I received a box full of doggie costumes. I laughed when I opened the box because I knew our dogs would never willingly wear those costumes. But that box sent my creative juices into a frenzy, and I came up with an idea for a great fund-raiser.

Many people over the years have expressed interest in visiting the sanctuary. While we do not operate like a local shelter with an every day open door policy, we wanted to share the experience of watching our pack with the people that have supported us over the years. I talked with Rick, Jessica, Charlotte, Kate, and Jordon, about putting on a show that would include some of our dogs dressed in the costumes we had received. Everyone had wonderful ideas, and the plans for The Bash began to take shape.

The first stage of the celebration involved a walk through of the sanctuary. Everyone would have the opportunity to meet the pack and explore the environment they love. We rented the local community center only a few blocks from the sanctuary, and the fashion show was to take place on the stage in that building. We hired a local restaurant to cater the event. Rick and both of our children hold black belts in Tae

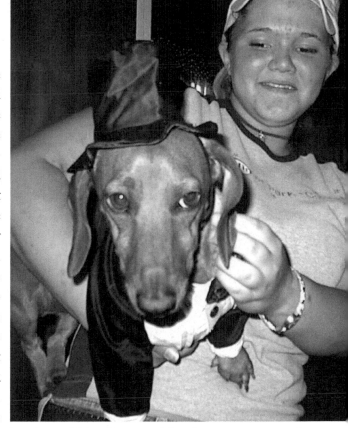

Kwon Do, and we thought it would be fun to add a demonstration of their skills to the evening. Everyone was excited about the entire plan, and then the real work began.

Rick and our son, Rick II, were put in charge of sprucing up the yard and planning the demonstration. Jessica and Jordon would help me prepare the inside of the sanctuary for our guests and coordinate transports of the dogs to the community center. Kate began work on the promotional aspects of the event with a page on our website, and Charlotte put out the word to all of our rescue contacts, our adoptive families, and the local news organizations. I had the job that turned out to be the most fun of all: I got to decide which dogs I wanted to participate and which

costumes they should wear.

Jordon volunteered to dress the dogs in their costumes. We needed three vehicles to transport the dressed dogs to the community center. I was in charge of receiving the dogs and lining them up for their stage appearances. Rick would serve as our Master of Ceremonies, and he planned to talk about the history of each of the dogs as well as some of their habits and quirks. After the fashion show, our meal would be served while the guys performed some of their Tae Kwon Do patterns and demonstrated their techniques of breaking boards and bricks with their hands and feet. We would finish the evening with an open auction of some beautiful handmade items that had been donated from all over the south.

The excitement in the air the morning of the Bash had everyone, including the dogs, a little on edge. I worried about how the dogs might react to an invasion of people. Xera and Macy concerned me the most. We determined that they should not participate in the walk-through. Xera would likely be overstimulated from all the new smells, and we did not want to have to warn all our guests to walk around with their hands behind their backs to accommodate Macy.

When our guests began to arrive around 4:00 p.m., Jessica and I greeted them on the porch. We led them into our entryway, which is separated from our living area by another door, five or six at a time. We wanted to ensure that both doors leading out of the house would not be open at the same time, keeping all our resident Dachshunds safely inside. Within just a few minutes our living room filled up with people. André and Gus greeted everyone, and instantly the entire pack began to flow through the house. By 4:30 p.m. our home and yard filled with people, and the dogs soaked up the attention.

Opal Ann brought out one of her tennis balls and encouraged everyone to throw it for her; Patch waggled from one person to the next, nose butting their shoes until they picked her up; the Rat Pack and Gus began to race down the yard; and Charlie worked at digging in his mine. The entire sanctuary came alive with giggles, conversations, and questions. Cameras flashed from every corner of the yard and house. Mia was passed from one hand to the next, soaking up the admiration; Sugar and Nate struggled to stay close to my heels; and Gracie rushed around trying to keep Patch rounded up. Rick carried Xera out into the kitchen to allow her supporters to see her. She responded better than I had hoped, and enjoyed

lots of love while still safe in Rick's arms.

By 5:30 p.m. we encouraged everyone to head over to the Community Center, and we started our fashion show at 6:00 p.m. The transports of the dogs worked out great because of the children volunteers who rode in the vehicles holding the dogs. André started the show in his tuxedo and top hat, Eddie impressed everyone in his jean jacket and leather biker's hat, Freddie was our cowboy,

Baby Jade amazed as a Geisha Girl, Christy crossed the stage in her General's outfit, Mia wore a beautiful pink Princess costume, Gus was dressed as Superman with his cape flowing over his wheel cart, JR made his appearance as a fireman, Sugar swayed across the stage in a grass skirt and lei, Jefferson wore a prison outfit, Nate was perfect in his sombrero and poncho, Dudley donned a cowboy hat and a vest with a badge, Heidi Louise filled out her cowgirl outfit perfectly, Milo dressed

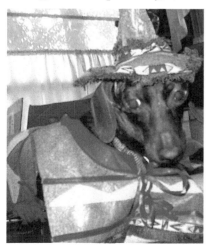

as a little elf, Gracie looked lovely in her white nurse's uniform, Ida Mae tried to shed her Santa outfit, Levi wore a pirate's costume, Phoenix drew a lot of attention in his pumpkin suit, and Patch was the only one I even considered for the devil costume. Nineteen of our residents appeared in costume that evening, and they brought the house down.

The entire event took the better part of five hours, and all of our hard work paid off. We made enough money to bring our current vet bill down to a zero balance, and we put enough back to cover our vet expenses through most of the rest of that year. Everyone in attendance loved meeting the dogs they had read about on our website. Quite a few rescuers that had been involved in our efforts up to that point were able to check out the dogs they had sent our way. And a few people that scoffed at our idea of a sanctuary, where all the dogs lived together, changed their attitudes toward our policies.

One hundred and eight people walked through our sanctuary that afternoon, and our caterer fed ninety-five guests at the Community Center. When our event ended, we were all exhausted. The dogs enjoyed all the extra attention but seemed pleased that our lives went back to normal

the next morning. We made quite a few new friends that day and acquired several new regular donors. One couple wrote three different checks during the event as they became more and more impressed with our process. It truly was a Bash to be remembered.

Chapter 14
Loud Noises and Other Spooky Stuff

Most of our dogs are afraid of one thing or another. Every once in awhile, a dog that others might perceive as fearless ends up acting like a baby in the face of something that should not be frightening at all.

Jake, one of our resident non-doxies, is courageous when it comes to protecting us or our property from strange dogs. He has also been resolute in the face of unfamiliar people. When I discovered some of the things my king sized dog is alarmed about, I was amazed. Jake is the only dog we have ever owned that is afraid of a water bowl. The kind we use have the big bottles that you turn upside down on the base. The air bubbles rush up to the top of the bottle sporadically, and Jake scrambles when they do. I believe he would literally starve himself of water if he had to drink from one of those containers. Another horrifying contraption in Jake's mind is my printer. When it beeps and begins to print, he can't get far enough away from it. The same thing happens when I turn on the vacuum cleaner. Some of our dogs attack the vacuum cleaner, a few of our dogs ignore the vacuum cleaner, but Jake hits the doggie door at full speed to escape that dreadful sucking monster. The absolutely most hilarious thing that upsets Jake is a sneeze. His nails slide and search for traction on our tile floors when I sneeze. Poor Jake suffers more than me when I get a cold! *Who would have guessed it?*

Many things can affect our dogs in many different ways. Sirens, however, produce an almost universal reaction at the sanctuary. It makes sense that all of our dogs could hear a siren at the same time. But the dogs often react in a sort-of round-robin. They are divided into five different areas. One section starts howling, another begins shortly after, and then it spreads. In just a few moments, all five groups are baying at the top of their lungs. Eventually, the first set of dogs get quiet, which causes a chain reaction in the others. *Another round, anyone?*

A couple of our dogs don't react at all to sirens. Xera never did. We originally wrote that off as her not being able to hear the noise, but other deaf dogs join in with the chorus. Mini hears very well but never howls at sirens. Cassie is the same way. *Could the fact that these two dogs are the least social dogs in the sanctuary have anything to do with that?* Some people think that dogs are reverting to their roots as wolves when they howl together. They are communicating with distant packs. *If that is true, I guess Mini and Cassie have nothing to say.*

Most research supports the theory that sirens do not hurt dogs' ears. The studies argue that if the sirens hurt their ears, they would be more likely to run and hide than to throw their snouts to the sky and join in. Most of our dogs revel in this activity. Delilah, on the other hand, gets frantic and tries to crawl all over us while she wails.

Birds can also produce a variety of responses from our dogs. Many different species of birds make their homes in the trees around our property. Some dogs bark at the birds, while others actually stalk them. Maxine

chased the shadows of birds flying across the yard. When their flight path left her sight, she dug a small hole. *Did she think those birds had gone underground?*

In our community, we have a flock of small quaker parrots who have escaped domestication. Their squawks are quite different from the sounds of the indigenous birds in our area. Gidget, our long hair Chihuahua, frantically hides when she hears these parrots. She never responds to the mockingbirds or the doves. She is not afraid of the hawks, or the grackles, but those parrots certainly have their bluff in on her.

Thunder is another element of our lives that elicits a comprehensive reaction. Most of our dogs scurry for cover when a storm grows close. Baby Jade reacts to the rumbling booms with the voracity of a rented mule heading back to the stable. She runs to the porch, ducks her head under the nearest blanket, and then plows across the porch dipping under every blanket until she has five or six piled on her back. I assume the blankets get heavy enough to weigh her down, and that's where she stays until the storm passes.

One evening, as a thunderstorm rolled in from the west, Baker displayed his expert athleticism, as well as his unbridled panic, as the thunderbolts lit up the sky. He ran full force across the lawn and launched himself into the open window of Rick's huge truck. He never touched the windowsill of that truck but landed safely inside. *Nothing but net!*

Gena runs to the bedroom and makes every effort to stuff herself under the bed during an electrical storm. She can only get the front half of her body tucked into that safety zone; the back half is left to fend for itself.

The Fourth of July is perhaps the hardest time of year for all of our animals that fear loud noises. Living outside the city limits means fireworks are permissible in our area. Unfortunately, they start two or three days early, and they can still be heard two or three days later. We can count on a full week of high anxiety. Rick's horses join our dogs in their repulsion of fire crackers. They bolt around the pasture, stomping and kicking until they realize the futility of their actions and head for the safety of the corral. Some of our neighbors have a reputation for putting on quite a show. Rick and I generally sit outside in our lawn chairs and are treated with awe-inspiring displays. None of our dogs join us for this event. They are all tucked under or behind their sanctum of choice.

One of the sillier reactions to "spooky stuff" involves Christy and our television. Rick and I are big fans of nature shows. We watch programs about wildebeest roaming the Serengeti or migrations of elk herds in Yellowstone. One recent show detailed the fighting among male lions in Africa for domination of their pride. Christy sat on the end of the bed staring at the television. Her head turned back and forth, as she obviously tried to digest what she saw. But when the battle began, she bolted back to Rick's side and squirmed her way under his covers.

Our pack never fails to entertain us. We certainly don't ever want them to be frightened of anything, and we make every effort to comfort them anytime they get spooked. But once in awhile, a few of them are so silly that we just have to laugh.

Chapter 15

Incumbents

This book could not be complete without a chapter on the current residents of the sanctuary Many of these dogs are not Dachshunds, but they are all deserving of a better life.

Charleen came to us as a puppy. She was born into a litter of mixed breeds that were being given away. Rick had recently lost Nipper, who had spent her entire life as his truck dog. Jessica and I picked Charleen up to help him move on from his grief over Nipper's death. Charleen became Charlie, and she grew quickly into the job of truck dog. By the time she reached four months old, she could jump into the cab of Rick's truck.

Charlie also patrolled our acreage like a dog on a mission. Skunks are a huge problem for us and our neighbors who raise chickens. Charlie holds the distinction of the best skunk hunting dog we have ever owned. Many times she came slinking up after a perimeter check, smelling from the consequences of her battles. Charlie has been with us for sixteen years. She no longer hunts skunks, and arthritis has taken her ability to climb up into Rick's truck. But Charlie sleeps on her blanket beside the bed each night and enjoys all the luxuries of her tenure here at the sanctuary.

André came to us as the first official rescue of The Promised Land. He was approximately one year old when he found himself in the local shelter. At sixteen, André is still here with us today.

Patch came to us during the first year of our sanctuary. Her influence over the lives of our other dogs has been tremendous. She is now fourteen

and as mischievous as ever.

Baby Jade is approaching her fourteenth birthday, but she still enjoys a youthful appearance. Thunder remains her biggest nemesis.

Colton came to us from a rescue friend in New Mexico. He was suffering from back issues and needed weeks of kennel rest. Colton did not fight the kennel like many of the dogs we were forced to isolate in this way. He relaxed and slept and chewed on his rope, content to watch the others from his haven. Colton's back healed completely, and he joined the pack as a middle aged Dachshund. He, thankfully, has not experienced any more problems with his back and will soon celebrate his thirteenth birthday.

Pete and Lucy, our mother and son duo, came from a local Dachshund breeder as cast offs because of their genetic problems. Lucy's face grows more gray with each passing day. She has a favorite sunny spot in the yard, and she spends her nights cuddled up with her son. Pete seems to defy time. His chocolate coat is still as beautiful as ever, and his bark is strong enough to raise the dead.

Christy is the current monarch of our lives. She is the sixth in a long line of Christies that began fifty-seven years ago, when Rick was just a small boy living in New Mexico.

Jake is my heart dog. It had been years since we had a German Shepherd when I rescued Jake from a local shelter. I found him sitting in a pen opposite a tiny Chihuahua that would not stop barking. Jake sat close to the door of his kennel, calm and quiet despite the ruckus. I placed my hand on the outside of his kennel, and he placed his paw on the fence to meet my hand. It was love at first sight for me. Jake is a longhair, and at ninety-three pounds, he has grown into the largest German Shepherd I have ever owned.

While walking Jake one day, a neighbor's dog decided to challenge us. Jake stayed close by my side and watched for any reaction from me. I tried to ignore the approaching dog, but when it continued to charge I quickened my pace. Jake took that as a sign for action. His six-inch-long hair stood out all over his body, which made him appear to be almost two feet wide. Jake leaped straight up into the air and turned a full hundred and eighty degrees to face the rushing dog. The minute his feet hit the ground, Jake roared like a lion. The approaching dog, not surprisingly, realized he had something to do elsewhere.

Gena is Jake's dog. Jake, as the only large dog residing in the house with us needed a partner. I saw Gena's picture on the website of one of our shelters, and decided to rescue her. Gena is a magnificent gold and black German Shepherd with a no-nonsense personality. She and Jake bonded easily and enjoy hours of playing and running in the yard every day.

Delilah also came into our lives from the local shelter. She is a top notch mouser and acrobat, despite the loss of her front right leg. Delilah is a bird dog mix, and her diva attitude, is unsurpassed in our pack. *Maybe… maybe not. Top diva in our pack is a highly contested position.*

Cassie wondered onto our property on Thanksgiving Day in 2012 and had a litter of puppies under an old tank by our horse corral. We discovered her and her puppies shortly after they were born, and immediately began to feed her. After several weeks, I went to the corral one morning to let the horses out, and Cassie was gone. I could still hear her puppies crying under the tank but could not locate their mom. When we did not see any sign of Cassie's return that evening, Rick crawled under that tank to rescue her puppies. When he retrieved six, I prayed that would be all. When he reached eight, I struggled to keep them all rounded up. By the time he had pulled out ten puppies, I laughed to keep from crying.

We placed the puppies in an empty pen behind our house. They were old enough to eat kibble, and we felt they could survive despite being apparently abandoned so early in their lives. But the next day when I tended to the horses, I spotted Cassie wondering in the pasture, no doubt searching for her puppies. I called her to me and placed her in my vehicle. When I drove up by the pen that held her puppies, Cassie stood up in the seat and whined. She ran for that pen the minute I opened the door. Cassie is a solid white Labrador/shepherd mix, and all ten puppies looked just like her. Over the next few months, we were able to place all of her puppies in good homes, and Cassie is a sweet and gentle member of our pack.

Baker came into our lives during a particularly horrible rain storm. Rick saw him on the side of a busy road on the way to work. He pulled over, and Baker ran to the truck and jumped into the cab, soaking wet. His deep brown eyes poured out love and dedication for Rick from the very beginning of their friendship. Baker assumed Charlie's role as Rick's truck dog when Charlie retired. Baker is, without question, one of the smartest dogs we have ever owned. He understands and responds to every word Rick says. We believe Baker is a Red Heeler/Labrador mix, and his cinnamon coat is spotted with white.

Little Bit is a tiny, red Dachshund with one of the prettiest faces we have ever seen. She was found locked inside the backyard of an empty house. Little Bit had been living inside an old pillow during a record breaking cold spell. The cook of a nearby restaurant heard her cries, and pried the gate open. For over a week, that kind man fed her a few scraps each day. Unsurprisingly, Little Bit's physical condition was not ideal. Her hair was coarse and dull, and we felt it was a miracle she had survived eight straight days of single digit temperatures. Rick brought her home tucked inside his coat, and I fell in love as quickly as he had. Within a few weeks, she was completely vetted and completely spoiled. Her coat now shines like a new penny, and she never has to worry about being cold again.

Mini is a chihuahua that I pulled from a local shelter. Her ears are constantly standing at attention, and they are almost as big as she is. Mini is somewhat of a loner, and her bark sounds more like a slow revving engine than that of a dog.

Gidget is a gorgeous, longhair Chihuahua that Rick found in the middle of the road just a few blocks from our home. She had no collar and her tiny body was covered with ticks and fleas. We bathed her right away and treated the bugs. Gidget blossomed into a stunning little dog who fears nothing, except the parrots, of course.

Beth, a black and tan Chihuahua, and Dora, a blonde Dachshund, were extremely ill with a relentless case of kennel cough. They were in a local shelter about to be put down when one of the workers called me. After seeing Doc Jess, they spent five weeks in isolation before we felt they were well enough to join the pack. Beth is young and ornery, Dora is probably around ten years old, and has lost most of her eyesight to cataracts.

Noel had the misfortune of finding herself in the middle of a downtown street. Fortunately for her, Rick came out of a nearby business just in time to run out in traffic and scoop her up out of harms way. She is a Chihuahua/Pug mix that stole our hearts on Christmas Eve 2013. After the loss of our sweet Opal Ann, Rick did not believe he would ever have another dog that loved to fetch as much as Opal Ann. Noel proved him wrong.

Winston was another dog that was unfortunate enough to be locked in a backyard of an empty house. One of Rick's colleagues at work found him and brought him to Rick. *Gee, I wonder how he knew Rick would take another dog.* Winston is a terrier mix, with wiry black and gray hair. He and Noel are partners in crime and partners in the nightly game of fetch.

Grace (not to be confused with Nurse Gracie) a medium size Pit Bull mix, found herself walking a railroad track close to Rick's workplace. Unfortunately, that track runs along a busy highway. Rick chased her for half an hour, and she narrowly escaped the wheels of several huge oil field trucks. *And you guessed it, she now has a permanent home here at the sanctuary.*

Dakota is a beautiful, but slightly crazy, German Shepherd pulled from the local shelter. To my surprise, she had been in that cage for almost a week with no inquiries. Dakota had run out of time. I did not hesitate, and by late afternoon she was resting in one of our pens.

Rick, as was his custom, wanted to meet and greet Dakota when he arrived home late that evening. It was dark outside when he approached the pen. Dakota shocked Rick by rushing the gate when he opened it, and she disappeared into the darkness. We both drove all over our area for several hours before we had to give up looking for her. For the next few days, I drove every street in our little country community, searching for her. *It's difficult to call a dog that doesn't know her own name.*

We soon experienced one of the worst ice storms this part of West Texas has ever seen. Power lines broke and fell, and tree branches covered the yards and streets. Everything shut down for three days until the sun finally came out and began to melt the ice. Once the roads became passable, I placed fliers with Dakota's picture in all the local vet offices, on the bulletin board of our local post office, online, and at the shelter where I found her.

We received a few calls saying Dakota had been sighted, but we were never able to find her. After six weeks, we hoped she had found a new home, and we stopped pursuing her. That's when we received a phone call from Diane. She had seen Dakota's story posted online, and then by chance saw a German Shepherd running the loop around town. She stopped and Dakota did not hesitate to jump into her truck. I had little hope that Diane had actually found Dakota, but I went to investigate anyway. When I walked into that backyard, and Dakota approached me, I felt my heart jump into my throat. The picture I had taken in the shelter assured Diane that Dakota was the dog I had lost, and she allowed me to bring her home.

The next day Dakota visited Doc Jess, and along with being spayed, and vaccinated, we had her microchipped. Dakota has been with us now for two years. We still wonder how she managed to survive that ice storm, live on her own for six weeks, catch the eye of a part-time rescuer online, and then end up on the loop in time to catch a ride with Diane.

Striker is a black, mixed breed that lived a perilous life on the truck yard where Rick worked. Rick tried for several weeks to catch Striker, but his efforts were in vain. One day he managed to get Striker cornered in a truck bay that was half full of water. Rick reached for him but missed. Striker misjudged his escape and got his head caught between the wall and a pipe. Rick was able to grab him. That frightened dog struck out and pierced Rick's nose with his teeth, but ended up in the truck anyway. Striker, after a year and a half, still does not want to be touched. But he enjoys the yard, the regular food, the absence of huge trucks to dodge, and the friends he had found at the sanctuary.

Millie is a gorgeous black and tan Dachshund with ears that dwarf most Dachshunds'. She came to us from a friend of a friend at Rick's work. Millie displays symptoms of being obsessive, but she gets along with our pack just fine.

Rudy came to us two days before Christmas in 2014, and Jessica named him Rudolph because of his red nose. Rick was called out to work and found Rudy along the side of a highway. He made an attempt to drive by, telling himself we didn't need to bring home another dog. But Rudy needed to be rescued off that highway in the middle of nowhere, and his needs prevailed. He is a sweet red Dachshund that obviously appreciates his new home. He and Striker have formed a strong bond that has been very beneficial to Striker.

Jaxson is a small German Shepherd that I took on as a favor to Doc Jess. He was born with mega-esophagus and a heart condition. His previous owners did not feel they were capable of taking care of him. Jaxson, unfortunately, also suffers from emotional issues. He came to us a bit aggressive toward other dogs and men. It didn't take long for Rick to win him over, however. I felt like Jaxson was completely obsessed with himself and needed a partner. At seven-months-old, he had never been socialized with other dogs. Rick and I knew that our adult German Shepherds would not tolerate his attitude.

Caring for his physical ailments was something we already knew how to do. Jaxson is now a year and a half old, has never had pneumonia, and is slowing gaining some height and weight. His psychological needs, like several other dogs we loved, required the help of another dog. He needed to grow up with a female puppy.

Valentine (Val) was rescued as a therapy dog for Jaxson. I ran into a couple outside the local shelter that had six Labrador mixed puppies they intended to leave. The puppies' mom had an encounter with a handsome stranger and delivered ten puppies. They managed to place four puppies in permanent homes, but had no way of handling the other six. I picked out one of the females, brought her home to introduce to Jaxson, and they have grown devoted to each other. Val has proven to be the answer to Jaxson's emotional issues, and she is teaching him how to be a happy dog.

Red and Ranger provided the most challenging rescue that Rick has ever pulled off. They also showed up at the truck yard and were obviously bonded to each other. Red is a beautiful male Heeler, and Ranger is a

medium sized female Shepherd mix. Several attempts at trying to pet them failed. Red bared his teeth and growled if he felt threatened, and he was extremely protective of Ranger. Weeks of trying to befriend these two wild dogs turned into months.

When the truck drivers complained, Rick grew increasingly desperate to rescue Red and Ranger. He attempted to catch them inside his horse trailer. Parked behind Rick's shop, the trailer provided a sheltered area to feed the dogs. After becoming accustomed to the easy meals, Red and Ranger decided to get into the trailer to eat. Rick tried to close the door with both dogs inside, but Red is clever, and ran for daylight. Rick opened the trailer, and Ranger followed Red to safety.

The following week, the boss allowed Rick two days to get the job done before he planned to call the dog catcher. I made a call to Doc Jess and got a few of her nighty-night pills. Rick added those pills to the dogs next meal, and soon they were both docile enough for Rick, with the help of a few friends, to get them into the truck. We met at the vet clinic, and they kept Red and Ranger sedated long enough to alter and vaccinate them.

These dogs now live in our barn. They have a new doghouse, plenty of food and water, and seven horses to bark at. Red now lives for attention, and he wraps his arms around Rick in a bear hug each day, thanking him for their new lives. Ranger is a perpetual puppy: running, jumping, and throwing dirt clods in the air. They act like they have been with us all their lives.

Cooper is a white chihuahua that my sister's grandson rescued off the streets. He didn't really have a good place to keep his new dog, so Cooper ended up in a kennel for ten hours a day. They wanted to find him a good home, and they did. Cooper now competes with Winston for the position of Noel's best friend and fetching partner.

It is blatantly obvious that everyone that knows us, knows we are not capable of saying no to a dog in trouble. Unfortunately, there has never been a shortage of dogs that need a permanent home. Rick and I have resigned ourselves to always having a rather large pack. I am never surprised when he brings home a new dog, and he isn't shocked when I bring one home from the vet or the shelter. God has a way of putting these dogs in our path, and thankfully, he provides the blessings we need to care for them.

Chapter 16

To All the Dogs We Loved Before

I could not write this book without paying homage to some of the dogs we loved before we became an official rescue organization. Those dogs who embraced us, who watched our children grow up, and who filled our lives with wonder and joy, helped mold us into the people we always wanted to be.

Christy Vaughn Eicher, III, IV, and V had all been integral parts of our lives, before our first official rescue in 2001. These cherished, influential Dachshunds will forever hold a special place in our hearts. All of Rick's friends and family accepted the fact that if you invited Rick over, Christy was coming with him. When our niece married in our home soon after we moved to the country, Christy IV attended the wedding. Even the preacher acknowledged her presence, and the entire audience

laughed. *No one doubted she had received her own personal invitation to the festivities.*

B.B., a beautiful, black and silver German Shepherd, came with me into our marriage. I raised her from a puppy, and she had been a wonderful part of my life for four years. B.B. had a majestic head and perfect German Shepherd conformation. She escorted our children around our large backyard in town from the time they were toddlers. I remember one day watching B.B. and the kids through the window in my kitchen. She was attempting to herd the kids away from a storage building in the backyard. No matter how hard they tried to get past her, she managed to place herself between them and that old brick building. I decided to investigate, and I found a large yellow jacket wasp nest under one of the awnings. B.B. proved to be an excellent babysitter, and we all loved her until her last day at the age of nine.

After we moved to our country home in August of 1984, we very much enjoyed the privacy that having no next-door neighbors, provided. That seclusion, however, brought with it an isolation factor that we soon discovered could be frightening. Our new home sat in the middle of a pecan orchard. When the pecans began to fall, truckloads of people showed up. They wanted to harvest pecans, and a few times they refused to leave when I asked them to.

Rick and I decided it was time to beef up our defenses. Sasha, an amazing German Shepherd, came into our lives as a ten week old puppy. Full of energy and ingrained savvy, Sasha soon learned the lay of the land. She followed the kids and me while we worked in the orchard. Sasha continually circled the area where we worked, setting up a perimeter that she fully intended to defend. By the time pecan season rolled around again in the fall of 1985, Sasha had grown into a force to be reckoned with.

One day just before Thanksgiving, I arrived home to find our front drive crowded with uninvited pickers. I asked them to leave, but the only response I received came in the form of giggles from a few of the young men. They had already begun to fill sacks with pecans from our yard. I immediately went inside and grabbed Sasha by the collar. When I stepped out onto the drive with her, the ladies and young girls all rushed to their vehicles. The young men continued to help themselves to our crop.

After my request for them to leave again fell on deaf ears, I released Sasha. She charged, baring her teeth, and growling like a bear. *Now we had their attention!* The last three stubborn fools scrambled to jump into the back of one of their trucks. But Sasha did not stop her pursuit until those men were standing on top of the cab of their truck; Sasha had jumped right up into the bed. I called her off and she reluctantly returned to my side on the porch. Seconds later, all of our unwelcome guests drove away. I was the only one giggling when Sasha and I went inside.

For the next ten years, Sasha guarded our land, our children, and me every day. She was the first and most effective security system we ever loved.

Casey, a rambunctious Scottish Terrier puppy, came into our lives as a Christmas present for Jessica in 1988. At only seven weeks of age, Casey already resembled a little tank. She loved to chase Jessica through the house and yard, biting at her shoes or socks. Casey and Christy became

good friends, but Casey's only true love was Jessica. She comforted Jessica through her emotional teenage years, and she waited patiently for her return each time Jessica left the house.

Casey developed a habit early in her life that never failed to make us all laugh. She approached bugs on the porch or in the yard and turned her head from side to side. She wanted to get the full measure of the creature. Then Casey reared back, and slammed the side of her head against the bug. Occasionally, it took more than one blow to get the job done. Casey persevered. I worried a bit that she might be causing some damage to her brain by this violent action, but she continued to do it her entire life. She suffered no ill effects, as far as we could tell.

Jessica remembers that Casey barked at any boys that made the mistake of sitting down on her bed. Jessica's husband, to this day, swears that Casey had a mean streak. Casey yearned for Jessica when she went away to college. Each time Jessica visited that first year, Casey seemed to know she was coming. She could be found waiting in the living room for Jessica, just as she had done for all those years before. Casey made her final journey at the age of eleven, and our Christy fainted on her pillow when Rick pulled Casey's lifeless body from under the bed. Christy's reaction to the loss of her sweet friend was our first lesson in the power of a dog's grief. The entire family felt the loss of that funny Scottie, but Jessica still misses her loving, quirky bud.

Rick found Nipper sitting under a mesquite tree on the side of the highway. Nipper stood just above knee high, and her body and legs were long and lanky. She could run as fast as any large dog we ever owned. Our son, Rick II, approached Nipper sitting in the den one day. He had a tape measure in his hand, and I watched to see just what he planned to measure. His discovery became part of our standard description of Nipper. Her legs measured sixteen inches, the length of her body was twenty-one inches, and yet Nipper could sit in a six inch square with a little room to spare. Nipper loved Rick. She spent every second that Rick was home beside him or riding in his truck. Nipper began a legacy of truck dogs for Rick that included some of the most memorable dogs that have blessed our lives. Charlie filled Nipper's spot after we lost Nipper at the age of eleven. Charlie retired after fourteen years, and Baker is now in his third year as the official truck dog.

Homer wondered onto our property, covered with ticks and matted hair. Rick and I knew the best way to help this little white fur ball would be to shave off those matts, and treat him for the pests. Once we finished our unprofessional grooming job, Homer looked like a hairless cat. Soon his coat grew back in, and we managed to keep the matts under control. Homer's underbite made him look like a bulldog in the face. His long ears flapped against his head when he ran, and we all adored him. Any

indication of danger sent Homer into an unrivaled barking escapade. Any challenge to his manhood sent him into a tail spin that only ended once he reached the security of the porch. We didn't know for sure how old Homer might have been when he joined our family, but we laughed at and loved that little guy for another twelve years.

Tootsie actually belonged to a family that lived down the road. She came to visit us each time the neighbor kids came to play. Tootsie played with Sasha and enjoyed many sessions with Rick scratching her belly until she moaned with delight. Tootsie was a pit bull that never showed any sign of aggression toward animals or humans. At some point, Tootsie ended up in the dog catchers truck. When Rick found out, he informed her owners. Everyone agreed that Rick should pull Tootsie from the shelter, and she would be our dog. And when I say our dog, I actually mean Rick's dog. Tootsie joined a long line of dogs that lived for Rick's scratching and affection.

Rambo was a horse. Well, actually, he was a Rottweiler/Doberman mix that stood almost as tall as our little Welsh pony. A friend of Rick's found himself in a situation that required Rambo, or Bo as we called him, to be re-homed. His size and suspicious nature commanded respect from everyone that laid eyes on him. Bo never charged at strangers. Instead he stood his ground, waiting to react to any threatening moves.

Bo and Tootsie became running buddies. In fact, Tootsie could run under Bo and never touch his belly. It didn't take Tootsie long to discover that there wasn't a safer place than when she was completely shaded by that giant dog. At one hundred and thirty-five pounds, Bo weighed about twenty pounds less than Rick. He could only be controlled by respect for his owner, and thankfully he held Rick in high regard.

Rex, a playful, mischievous German Shepherd; Monte, a silly, but powerful Doberman; Chance, a lovable, large mixed breed; Samantha, a gracious, intelligent Labrador; and Benji, a red, long-hair Dachshund, also blessed our lives with their devotion. I have a little plaque hanging in my home that says, "Dogs are not our whole life, but they make our lives whole." *Truer words, have never been spoken.*

Epilogue

Our incredible story of rescue runs the full gambit of emotions. Our successes brought more happiness to our hearts than we thought possible. That joy helped us heal each time our hearts were broken.

From July 2001, when we first established The Promised Land Dachshund Sanctuary, until February 2016, two hundred and fifty-eight dogs passed through our doors. While most dogs began a new chapter in our sanctuary before moving on to their own special homes, or establishing their place in our lives, there were others that we could not restore. Those stories are also victories because the dogs passed knowing someone loved them.

We loved them enough to pull them from high-kill shelters. We loved them enough to pull them from backyard breeders and established puppy mills. We loved them enough to pick them up off the streets. And, we loved them enough to take them from their previous owners who could no longer honor their commitments to their pets. The only possibility for failure was the failure to act.

The day we brought our first official rescue home, we knew we were facing a lifelong commitment. Many times over the years, we faced financial and emotional hurdles that frightened us or broke our hearts. It took only a few minutes in prayer and a few minutes watching our pack play to give us the strength and courage to continue.

While the opinions of others have always been a consideration for Rick and me, we were not willing to let them completely alter our path. Once, early in our efforts, we were wounded by some labels other rescuers placed on us. Perhaps the hardest portrayal to understand stemmed from our decision to keep Patch. We were called hoarders by a few people we thought we could trust.

The facts of our rescue do not support that label. One hundred and fifty-two dogs that we rescued were successfully adopted. All of the dogs that came through our lives received excellent vet care. Our accusers made full use of the sanctuary policy to accept every one of the seniors or special-needs Dachshunds that they needed to exclude from their programs. Thankfully, all of our regular supporters brushed off those ill-conceived complaints.

Double dapples made up a large portion of the dogs born disabled

that came through our door. I want to try and explain a little about the breeding practices that produce these dazzling but unfortunate dogs. Dachshunds can be naturally dappled, just as some breeds have naturally occurring merle coats. A dapple Dachshund will have splotches somewhere on its body of variegated color, and they carry a higher price tag. When two dapples are bred together, the result is double dapple puppies. Those puppies inherit a dapple gene from both parents, and the natural selection process will determine where on the dog's body those genes overlap. If they happen to overlap in the eyes, the puppy will be blind. If they happen to overlap on the ears, the puppy will be deaf. Double dapple Dachshunds ALWAYS produce dappled puppies, even when bred to a normal colored dog. Therefore, some breeders will risk a litter of disabled puppies to be able to breed one double dapple for life. *You do the math.*

Another disability that has played a role in our sanctuary is mega-esophagus. On-set of this debilitating condition can occur very early in a dog's life, or it can strike an adult dog. Proper feeding of dogs suffering from mega-esophagus has been in our experience, the most important factor that determines their chances at a full life. Mia and Milo enjoyed many more years than they were originally predicted to have. Our success with these two dogs led Doc Jess to ask us to take on Jaxson. *Plus she knew I could never refuse a German Shepherd in need.*

Dachshunds are also genetically prone to bad teeth. This can make their long term care quite expensive. Nevertheless, the dangers of infections in their mouths are substantial. Those infections can eat away the bone in their jaws, can spread through the sinus cavities to their brains, and can be picked up in the blood stream to damage the heart and other organs. Many of our rescued dogs came to us with flaming infections in their mouths. They lost most or all of their teeth.

Our stories have depicted the substantial risk for mammary and testicular cancer in unaltered dogs. Even if these dogs were not forced to produce litter after litter of puppies, leaving their reproductive organs intact causes a vast increase in their chances of having certain cancers.

The most significant risk that the dogs in our country face, however, is over-population. The latest numbers indicate that approximately three and a half million dogs enter animal shelters nationwide each year. More than half of those dogs are euthanized. Just over two billion dollars a year are spent in the U.S. to catch and euthanize stray animals. *Surely we can do better than this!*

Our situation at the sanctuary was drastically altered in August of 2005, when I became ill. For over two years, Rick bore a tremendous amount of the burden to continue to care for the dogs we both loved. We were forced to take down our website and discontinue our official rescue status. Rick was steadfast in his commitment to pulling me, and the thirty-four dogs in our sanctuary, through some difficult years. His strength and courage has been the single most important factor, aside from our blessings from above, to keeping our dream alive. Rick is one of the only true heroes I have ever known, and I am humbled by his dedication to me and all of God's creatures.

Today, I enjoy perfect health, and our rescue efforts continue. We don't have a wonderful website or a large group of supporters anymore, but we still do everything in our power to help the dogs in need that cross our path.

I have made every attempt by writing this book to bring you into the lives of the dogs we have known and cherished. Our hope is that readers will gain an understanding of the rescue world, the value of ALL dogs, and the responsibility we all share to reverse the tide of undervalued dogs of all ages and abilities.

Dogs are not disposable. Dogs love and learn, they play and tease, and they hope and grieve. Dogs give us everything they have. All they ask for in return is a small effort on our part to keep them safe and loved.

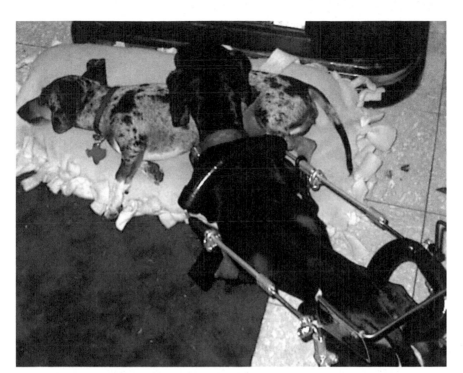

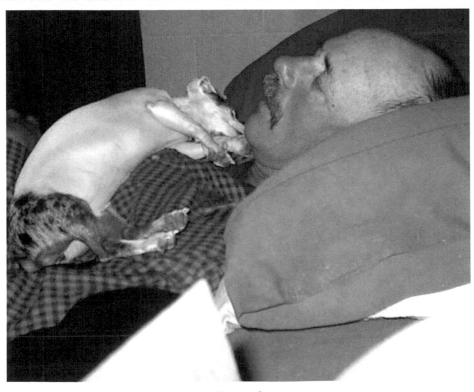

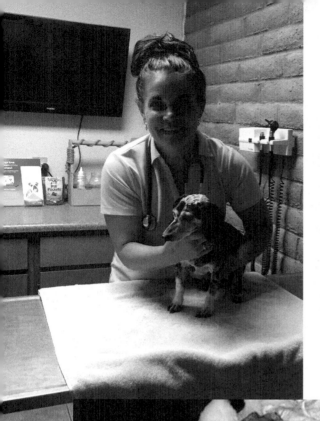

Please help us keep our sanctuary alive by donating to the care of our current residents and all those to follow.

Donate by PayPal to: promisedlanddachshund@yahoo.com

Donate Directly to our Vet Care Fund:
A-Z Vet Clinic
8535 W. Hwy. 158
Midland, TX 79707
1-432-520-8387

Mail Checks or Money Orders:
The Promised Land Dachshund Sanctuary
PO Box 826
Gardendale, TX 79758

Follow our blog: thepromisedlanddachshundsanctuary.org